THE TWO SIDES
OF A COIN

by

Charles ❤ Frances Hunter

Published by
Hunter Books
201 McClellan Road
Kingwood, Texas 77339

BOOKS BY CHARLES & FRANCES HUNTER

A CONFESSION A DAY KEEPS THE DEVIL AWAY
ANGELS ON ASSIGNMENT
ARE YOU TIRED?
BORN AGAIN! WHAT DO YOU MEAN?
COME ALIVE
DON'T LIMIT GOD
FOLLOW ME
GO, MAN, GO
GOD IS FABULOUS
GOD'S ANSWER TO FAT...LOØSE IT!
GOD'S CONDITIONS FOR PROSPERITY
HANDBOOK FOR HEALING
HANG LOOSE WITH JESUS
HIS POWER THROUGH YOU
HOT LINE TO HEAVEN
HOW DO YOU TREAT MY SON JESUS?
HOW TO HEAL THE SICK
HOW TO MAKE YOUR MARRIAGE EXCITING
HOW TO WIN YOUR CITY TO JESUS
HOW TO RECEIVE AND MAINTAIN A HEALING
HOW TO OVERCOME "COOL DOWN" AND KEEP THE FIRE BURNING
How to Receive and Minister THE BAPTISM WITH THE HOLY SPIRIT
I DON'T FOLLOW SIGNS AND WONDERS...THEY FOLLOW ME!
IF YOU REALLY LOVE ME...
IMPOSSIBLE MIRACLES
MEMORIZING MADE EASY
MY LOVE AFFAIR WITH CHARLES
NUGGETS OF TRUTH
POSSESSING THE MIND OF CHRIST
P.T.L.A. (Praise the Lord, Anyway!)
SINCE JESUS PASSED BY
the fabulous SKINNIE MINNIE RECIPE BOOK
STRENGTH FOR TODAY
SUPERNATURAL HORIZONS (from Glory to Glory)
THE TWO SIDES OF A COIN
THIS WAY UP!
VIDEO STUDY GUIDE - HOW TO HEAL THE SICK (14 Hrs.)
VIDEO STUDY GUIDE - HOW TO HEAL THE SICK POWER PACK (6 Hrs.)
VIDEO STUDY GUIDE - THE BOOK OF ACTS (11 Hrs.)
WHY SHOULD "I" SPEAK IN TONGUES???

EVERY FIVE OR TEN YEARS. . .

. . .a new figure appears on the scene, bringing something exquisitely timely.

This time the figure was a double portion as a dynamic couple appeared.

To our sin-weary depressed generation Charles and Frances Hunter have brought laughter and light.

They are established best-selling writers because of their sensitivity to the times. Each of their books have brought teaching and harvest to the body and the soul.

Hundreds of thousands have accepted the baptism with the Holy Spirit because of the experience related in THE TWO SIDES OF A COIN!

Scripture quotations are taken from:

The Authorized Version (KJV)
The New English Bible
The Living Bible, Paraphrased
(Wheaton: Tyndale House, Publishers, 1971).
All references not specified are from The Living Bible.

THE TWO SIDES OF A COIN

ISBN 0-917726-36-7

Library of Congress Catalog Card Number: 75-10605

Published by Hunter Books
201 McClellan Road, Kingwood, Texas 77339
Printed in U.S.A.

TABLE OF CONTENTS

CHAPTER 1

THE TWO SIDES OF A COIN

IT'S GENUINE, IT'S REAL, AND I'VE GOT IT!

I nearly screamed the words over the telephone after I had frantically dialed Charles.

It was real . . . and I KNEW IT!

It was genuine . . . and I KNEW IT!

It was of God . . . and I KNEW IT, because Jesus had given it to me. I had reached up and He had reached down and touched me another time—this time as the Baptizer. I thought I would never be able to contain myself because of this new reality of Jesus Christ. Did this really happen to me? Yes it did! Was it just an emotional happening or had a dramatic change occurred in my relationship to God?

Today I KNOW! What do I know? I know that a dramatic change occurred, not just a momentary emotional high of reaching God, but a beautiful, stablizing power-packed dimension was added at that moment when my very soul cried out from the depths of my innermost being asking God to prove the reality of a physical sign of the baptism with the Holy Spirit. That beautiful second when I was willing to meet God all the way—He sent Jesus to meet me right at my point of need! I knew it could change my life either way, and I had to be sure it was God's way and He showed me it was!

"God, when did you put all those new verses of scripture in the Bible?" I had never seen them before, and all of a sudden they began running through my mind—they had been there all the time! I just hadn't seen them! I hadn't listened when God was speaking to me! Then it all seemed so simple. Salvation plus commitment plus baptism equals victory in Jesus!

Heavenly Father,

How we love you, how we praise you, how we worship you, and how we thank you for giving the Holy Spirit to us, and for making Him so real in our lives. You know we're not theologians, we're just two ordinary people who love you very much, and we thank you for what you've done for us. We ask that those who read this book will know that we're not trying to present a theological dissertation, that we are only desirous of sharing what happened to us, and what a blessing this "happening" has been in our lives.

Father, we pray that everyone who reads this book will read it with an open heart and an open mind, and will let you speak to them through its pages. We'd also ask that ALL who read this book will go on to have a closer, more exciting and more personal walk with you.

Thank you for hearing our prayer.

Charles 💝 Frances

CHAPTER 2

BLINDED—BY FEAR
By Frances

In my kitchen hangs a happy looking plaque which says: "Lord, help my words to be gracious and tender today, for tomorrow I may have to eat them."

God knew what He was doing when He had me buy that! It's a good thing I don't mind eating my words, because that's just exactly what both Charles and I have had to do. Praise God! And what an exciting time we're having eating some of the things we've said over the past few years. No spiritual indigestion at all! Although when I first became aware of the fact I was going to have to eat a lot of things I had said, there might have been moments of panic when I envisioned a big spiritual stomachache! But not so; God in His beautiful love made it as painless as possible and His grace made it possible to be able to admit I'd been wrong!

I had really been blinded along the road of Christian growth just because I was afraid of something I really didn't know about! I was completely blinded to an additional dimension of God Himself because I was not willing to accept what He wanted to give me, but I love Him even more because He let me run the gamut of spiritual childhood without getting provoked at me. How loving and patient God is!

I was one of those individuals who was "born in the fire and never satisfied with dead ashes" and from the moment of accepting Christ as my Saviour there has been a compelling desire to tell people what God's love can do in their lives. When I finally accepted the fact that *God will do what He says He will,* I stood there and thought my heart was just going to burst right out of the walls of my body, because in that beautiful moment of the awareness of God's splendor and power, I was acutely aware of the fact that Jesus Christ was *personally* living in my heart. I remember lying in bed one night and as I looked down at my chest, I could see an extra strong heartbeat at that moment because I knew that it was no longer *my* heartbeat, but the heartbeat of Jesus Christ, LIVING IN ME! The awesomeness of that realization overwhelmed me, not only because He had come to live in my heart, but because He was willing to do the same thing for anyone who would simply invite Him to come in.

I think of all the years I spent in darkness, running after the pleasures of the world, thinking that the "fun" of the world was the answer to life—that the happiness I found in material things such as parties, dances, cocktails, escapades and the like, were the only things that were real and the only things that were fun. Looking back now and remembering the parties I used to have, I can see that each year it took a little more money, a little more energy, a little more alcohol, a little fancier food, a little more in the way of decorations and invitations, a little more strain and a lot more pretending to convince even myself that I had as good a time this year as we'd had at last year's party. If my annual Christmas party happened to be followed by a working day, we always judged the fun we'd had the night before by the miserable way we felt the day after. Practically everyone who came to the party would come into the office some time the next day, and we'd laugh (sometimes a little forced) at how miserable we felt.

I must be honest and admit that during those years I did have fun—*to the best of my knowledge at that time*—but I obviously didn't know very much. Remember, too, the Bible says that even sin is fun for a season! While I didn't realize that it had begun to pall, God did, and in the fullness of His perfect timing, He began drawing me to Himself.

I must honestly admit that as God began drawing the gossamer web of His love around me, the threads were so fine and delicate I didn't even see them coming. When He drew them tightly around me, I struggled for a while because I thought He was trying to bind me, but when I saw the beauty of what He was doing, I lifted my hands in total surrender. Never was there a partial surrender. With me, from the words "I believe", I wanted to give God everything I had, little realizing that what He promised in return was everything He had!

I HAD TO TELL THE WORLD! I looked at my martini-drinking friends and recognized the God-shaped vacuum in their lives and I remember saying, "God, am I going to have to save the whole world by myself?" I didn't realize there might be anyone else around because no one had ever spoken to me about my soul in the first 48 years of my life! And so I took off like a rocket, wondering how long it would take me to evangelize the world.

Before I became a Christian, I went to my pastor and asked him what our church stood for. Among other things, I remember he said, "We don't believe in tongues!" I said, "What's that?" I had never heard of anything like that, and so my introduction to this subject was given to me by someone I had learned to love and respect. I believed what he said, since he had taught me so much about God's love and the fact that Jesus Christ wanted to come and live His life through me. I don't honestly remember what his comment was except it concerned people who got carried away and spoke in some kind of gibberish which didn't make sense and which caused problems. And now I realize he believed this because this is what he had been taught. After that, tongues were a real "no-no" to me. After all, why shouldn't I believe what he taught? He had taught me the truth about being born again, so it was only natural that I should believe this part of his doctrine.

After I accepted Jesus as my Saviour and Lord, what a blast I had! I began sharing Christ with everyone who came into my office. I shared His love with the people I met at the filling stations, the grocery stores, even out on the streets. You can't start sharing your faith with everyone you meet without beginning to come in contact with Christians, too! I couldn't believe what was happening to me because I began receiving invitations to speak in churches of many different denominations. All I knew was I wanted to share Jesus with anyone who would listen to me.

My first real personal experience with tongues came as a result of my sharing my faith. I was invited to give my testimony in a certain church, and then give any unsaved in the congregation an opportunity to pray to receive Christ. I wonder now what I would have done had I realized in advance that this church spoke in tongues! I probably would have run as fast as I could in the opposite direction, but I didn't know anything about what kind of a church it was, so I went, happy in the knowledge I was going to get to share in my beloved Jesus.

Right after I got there I was told a traveling evangelist had just come by that day and they wanted us to share the service. They asked if I'd mind just taking 20 minutes or so, and sharing the rest of the time with him. In Christian love, I said, "Fine—they'll be getting a double portion tonight, won't they?" I gave my testimony first, and the congregation was very attentive. Then the "surprise" evangelist began to speak. A short talk on the Holy Spirit was given. I had been reading some books on the Holy Spirit at that time, but didn't quite understand everything he said. I was anxious to learn all I could, so I listened attentively. The evangelist asked all Christians to come to the altar and pray. I was wondering why when the two ladies who had escorted me to my seat said, "We'll take you up there, dear!"

Something within me reacted most peculiarly. As we started down the aisle, they flanked me on either side and a feeling of panic overtook me. As we reached the front pew, I dropped back, quickly turned around and knelt there, while they proceeded to the altar, not yet realizing they had lost me en route. I had a feeling I was where I shouldn't be, and was trying to figure out a means of escape. A young girl next to me was screaming, "Not my will, but thine!" All I could think of was, "This couldn't be God's will!" Talk about confusion, and talk about being scared! I wanted to run and get under a pew or something!

Then I really pushed the panic button. I heard the booming voice of the evangelist and as I looked up, he was coming straight for me! I felt like a cornered rat. I really would have panicked except for one thing—I KNEW that Jesus Christ was living in my heart, so I really called on the power of God! I sent up one of the fastest and most earnest prayers in history: "God, by the power of your Holy Spirit, I bind Satan right now in this place, because all I feel is evil. If what this man is going to do to me is not of you, stop him in the name of Jesus!" The evangelist looked as if he had slammed into an invisible brick wall. He turned and walked in another direction, and I got up and ran out of the building as fast as I could run. When I got outside and breathed the fresh air, I saw an interesting sign which said this evangelist had been there for one week already and would be there for a second week — not a "surprise" visit as they had told me. The Bible says to "try the spirits" and I had tried this one and didn't like what I found.

I was shaking from the experience, but managed to get in my car and drive to the parsonage where I shared with my pastor and his wife what I had just experienced. This really convinced me that what I had first heard about speaking in tongues was right, and we all rejoiced that we weren't involved in anything like this. I carried the horror of that night with me and any time the subject of "tongues" was brought up, it was like waving a red flag in front of a bull, and I really charged! I was convinced that anything that had to do with this subject was like what I saw that night, so it couldn't be of God. Notice how I judged the entire Holy Spirit movement by one meeting. I closed my mind to this issue and decided then and there this was not for me! How wrong can we be when we emphatically close the doors to anything of God without fully knowing the truth.

God had already begun spinning a little web around me again, but I didn't realize it because he did a very interesting thing shortly after that. Somehow He gave me an awareness of able to discern whether or not a person spoke in tongues. I remember how surprised I was to discover the interesting fact that within seconds after meeting a Christian, I could tell whether or not he spoke in tongues. This really intrigued me as God began to cross my path more and more with "beautiful" Christians with whom my spirit blended perfectly, even though I KNEW they spoke in tongues. There was perfect peace and love when I was with them, and a blending of spirits that was beautiful. Then I began to think how can this be? If it's as evil as I think it is, how can I KNOW positively that these people speak in tongues and yet their Christian love is beyond belief. I began to search a little more.

Can I share with you a question that has really bugged me many times? It wasn't really a question, but the attitude in which it was asked. Over and over again after I had shared in a service where the Spirit of the Lord had really been poured out and many people had found Christ, someone would come up to me and with a complete lack of love and haughtily ask, "Have *you* received the baptism with the Holy Spirit?"

I do not know of anything which can turn a person away from this beautiful gift of God faster than to have someone with a super superior attitude ask them this question! I finally began to give a standard answer, "Oh, yes, God has really baptized me with His Holy Spirit, but it isn't necessary to speak in tongues, if that's what you mean."

The look of condemnation on their faces as they looked down on me because I didn't carry the same "badge of spirituality" was unreal! I no longer was a sister in Christ! No longer did I have anything in common with them. I just wasn't on the same spiritual plane, being inferior because of not speaking in tongues. Many of these so-called "super-spiritual" Christians really seemed to be the ones Paul spoke of in I Corinthians 13:1: "If I had the gift of being able to speak in other languages, without learning them, and could speak in every language there is in all of heaven and earth, but didn't love others, I would only be making noise."

Then there have been those "beautiful" ones who in great love have asked me exactly the same question and when I gave exactly the same answer have said, "I hope you do some day," and we parted the best of friends with the Spirit of God communicating between us.

Shortly after this, some in my own church began receiving the baptism with the Holy Spirit. This didn't bother me too much because I was traveling a great portion of the time and was not often in my home church. It seemed to me many of the most exciting Christians were the ones who were receiving. I realize now it was those who were seeking more of God, and not those who were content just to warm the pews, who received the gift. Eventually most of those left the church quietly, without disturbance or confusion, since our church did not believe in this. I wrote to a friend of mine when I heard of their family leaving. They were the dearest of friends and I was grieved to see them go. Her letter in reply to me left no doubt at all that she was directed by God. I never knew why I saved that letter until now, but with her permission I am quoting it:

"Dear Charles and Frances:

"It was good to hear from you and catch up on some of your activities. Your new books sound exciting and I look forward to reading them. The next time you are in town I do wish you could spare a few minutes and come see us. We would really love to talk to you and share with you.

"I wasn't too surprised to hear from you about our leaving the church. We, too, have a special love for this church and the pastor. I don't profess to understand all the things that happen to us as we walk with the Lord, or why He deals with us in so many different ways. I do know we must be obedient to Him and I know you believe that with all your heart and soul, too.

"The Lord called us to the church and we had wonderful fellowship. Our two and a half years there blessed us in many ways and I hope we still have many dear friends there. But as the Lord called us to go there, He called us to leave. I'm not at all sure why it was at this time, but He knows, and it was a very definite call.

"We all want everything the Lord has for us and to walk closer to Him as He gives us more and more light. We are all faced with decisions each day and some of us choose one way and some another. All I can say is, I know, without any doubt, the Lord called us to leave the church. He didn't give us lots of reasons, but only asked us to obey. We have had complete peace about it all and of course, spent much time in prayer and listening to Him before we moved.

"Every day grows sweeter with Jesus. *Tongues is only a doorway to another experience with Jesus.* We, too, have seen the 'bad' side, but as with everything good from the Lord, the devil has a counterfeit. . . .Our spirit witnesses with this experience! Glory! Praise His Holy Name!

"We really would love to *really* share with you. We have a special love for you both and know the Lord is blessing your lives in a wonderful way. Please let us hear from you and try to see us when you're in town.

"All our love in His precious Name,"

I wrote back the day I received the letter and said, "I understand." And understand I did, because there have been many decisions God has required me to make which I didn't understand, nor did anyone else at the time. I only knew I had to be obedient to Him without counting the cost, and the beautiful Christian love in her letter said the same thing to me. She was doing what God had called *her* to do, and the blending of our spirits never waivered. Here was someone in whom I had seen all the fruit of the Spirit: love, joy, peace, patience, kindness, goodness, faithfulness, gentleness and self-control. That spoke to me lots more than those who forgot to speak in love. The letter didn't condemn me one single bit—it just loved me into a position of wanting to know more about what had happened to this beautiful sister in Christ.

CHAPTER 3

THE START OF A DESIRE—FOR CHARLES

By Charles

God uses exciting ways to get our attention and goes to seemingly endless extremes to teach us simple little lessons. I was amazed at the time and trouble God once went to with Jeremiah when he could have explained the whole illustration in about half a minute: Jeremiah 13:1-10 "The Lord said to me, Go, and buy a linen loincloth and wear it, but don't wash it—don't put it in water at all. So I bought the loincloth and put it on. Then the Lord's message came to me again. This time he said, Take the loincloth out to the Euphrates River and hide it in a hole in the rocks. So I did; I hid it as the Lord had told me to. Then, a long time afterwards, the Lord said; Go out to the river again and get the loincloth. And I did: I dug it out of the hole where I had hidden it. But now it was mildewed and falling apart. It was utterly useless! Then the Lord said: This illustrates the way that I will rot the pride of Judah and Jerusalem. This evil nation refuses to listen to me, and follows its own evil desires and worships idols; therefore it shall become as this loincloth—good for nothing."

Look at all the trouble God went to to illustrate this one point. He did the same thing to me. He set up a whole "teenage" problem to activate a desire that lay sleeping within me. God allowed the problem to arise and it shook our daughter Joanie to tears. I guess most of us keep having teenage problems all our lives—problems which seem at the moment to be like mountains, but in God's marvelous teaching process are just classroom situations He sets up to let us learn to trust Him.

Because of a one night gap in our tour itinerary, Joanie did not have our phone number. She had called our hostess the night before we arrived. Our tomorrow-hostess talked to Joanie just enough to know that she needed us urgently, that something very disturbing had happened, but did not press Joanie for details. About midnight we were located. We phoned our tear-soaked, frantic child. After talking a few minutes to Joanie and then talking to God, Joanie had all the peace she needed. As soon as she took her eyes off herself and her problem and put them on Jesus, she knew He would take care of everything.

Frances and I had just returned from our first Kathryn Kuhlman "miracle" service. As our hostess drove us back to her home, her face radiated the love of Jesus as she talked with us. There seemed something very special in her deep commitment. I asked her if she prayed in tongues. When she said yes, I wanted to hear how she received and what it meant to her. There was a genuineness about her that stirred within me a search for more truth about this subject. I'm sure God had already said, 'Charles, I have something I want to give you' and He had placed in the depth of my heart a desire to know more about it. She told us her story. I can only recall a little of the details, but when she finished I knew that what she had was good and that it was genuine.

She told us how she had prayed the night before when Joanie called her. As soon as she hung up the receiver after talking to Joanie, she went into her private prayer closet and started talking to God in her prayer language. She had no idea what the problem was so she did not know how to pray in English. She told us how she just let the Holy Spirit pray through her as she released herself, her tongue, her voice, her mind to His control. She said it seemed like she prayed only a short prayer but the clock registered a thirty minute private conversation with her heavenly Father—so private that even she was not aware of what she prayed, but she knew the wonderful completeness as she simply released herself and Joanie to God. She said a sincere fervency was constant as she prayed, and a peace came because she knew that God had heard.

God used this to impress me with this new dimension of prayer. Tongues were not an imaginary plaything, but instead were the means by which the Holy Spirit could pray through her for Joanie's need. This stirred within me an eagerness to experience this in my life!

CHAPTER 4

The Start of a
Desire—for Frances

By Frances

I don't honestly know when the first small but
real desire started in my heart. I wasn't aware of it
being a desire, or I might not have always obeyed the
Holy Spirit when He began to interest me about
reading books on this subject! I had been so ada-
mant in my thoughts I wouldn't even have a book in
my house that spoke on the positive side of the subject of tongues. Early in my Christian life I had read
a book called FACE UP TO A MIRACLE by Don
Basham and I remember thinking, "Well, that's fine
for him if he needs an experience like that, but I
don't because my life is already so exciting I can
hardly stand it." Probably as much as anything else
that kept me from reading the books was the way
they were presented to me, intimating that "I just
didn't have IT!" At times, as I went somewhere to
speak, someone would sneak a copy of THEY
SPEAK WITH OTHER TONGUES in my pocket-
book, or in my suitcase. Many times I've had 5 to 10
copies of this book given to me (secret service style)

while on a trip. As soon as I got to the airport, the first thing I did was TO DUMP THEM ALL IN THE TRASH CANS. (Charles says I'm really going to be surprised one of these days when one of the trash cans begins "speaking in tongues" when I walk by!) I wanted no part of anything that even remotely discussed this subject, let alone a book that came right out and approved of it. Self-righteously I drew myself "above" those people who needed this emotional stimulus!

Right after Pat Boone's book A NEW SONG came out, some friends in California asked Charles and me if we had read this book, and recommended it highly. We managed to pick up a copy in Los Angeles and I thought I'd glance through it on the plane on the way home. I couldn't put it down! I saw something I had never seen before: this was an added dimension to life, not as a "you've got to have this or you haven't got it" sort of thing. Here was a book that emphasized the GIVER and not the GIFT. I saw the beauty and the power of the baptism. I read and reread pages 110 and 111 about 25 times which tell of Shirley's baptism and I quote them for you here, because there is nothing I have ever read that says it better:

"God doesn't give us spiritual gifts just for our own enjoyment. Instead He gives us special abilities so that we can better worship and serve Him. That's where the real enjoyment is! This is what Jesus meant when He told the early disciples that they would be baptized with the Holy Ghost so that they might receive power—power to serve—power to overcome—power to become! This is why some Bible scholars have said, 'Don't seek the gifts, but the giver.'

"They're absolutely right! When our heart's desire is to have a closer relationship with Jesus Christ, above all other things, then we are in the best possible position to receive the Baptism in the Holy Spirit and the gifts He may provide. . ."

"Even though she didn't understand exactly what was happening, she prayed, 'Jesus, I need You—and only You. You said that if I ask for bread You wouldn't give me a stone. And if I ask for fish You wouldn't give me a serpent. I don't want anything from Satan, I don't want some psycological counterfeit. I'm offering you my voice, my lips, my soul, my life. I want to give all of me to You. I know Your Spirit has been *with* me, and in me, but please, dear Lord, now I need Your Spirit to fill me.

"If you have another language for me, I want it—but only if it's from You. I want you to baptize me in your Holy Spirit—as you promised.'

"And then when she'd said all she knew to say, she offered her voice, making soft sounds . . . knowing it was a step of faith, reaching out for Jesus. And He met her! . . . She was overcome by the sense of the presence of the Lord and overwhelming feeling of love.

"The amazing thing that happened to me was that I felt myself *immersed* in love. I don't know how else to explain it. We talk about being baptized or totally immersed in water. I was totally immersed in love. It was so beautiful."

I didn't realize it at the time, but God was putting Shirley's words into my mind to be recalled just about a year later.

Charles read the book as soon as I finished it, and he felt the same way I did. We wrote a letter to the Boones telling them how we enjoyed the book, and also sharing the fact that we really had been "turned off" on tongues. We are constantly cautioning people about not being legalistic, but rather encouraging them to let God work in and through them. Suddenly we saw something! "Look who's been legalistic all this time on this! I'm sure there have been many times when we've said to God, "We want EVERYTHING except tongues." How stupid could we have been! A NEW SONG made a tremendous impression on us.

Then God began spinning another part of His little web around us. I had been scheduled to speak at the Holy Spirit Teaching Mission in Miami, Florida. Just prior to this Charles and I were in the Pittsburgh area and we discovered we had a night free. This had never happened before. We looked in the paper to see what Christian speaker we might go to hear. We saw they were having a Charismatic Conference at a Presbyterian Church there. We both prayed and decided since I was going to be speaking at a Charismatic meeting in Miami it might be a good idea if we attended one here just to see what went on. I was still carrying in my mind what had happened in that church so long ago and so, apprehensively, we went.

When we went in, we made very sure we were

close to the exits because we knew that sometime during the meeting they'd start beating people on the head (we had always heard "they" did this—and isn't it ridiculous how we can believe things like this?), and we wanted to be in a good position for running, because we weren't going to let "them" beat us on the head! Then it began! And you'd never guess what happened! They sang some real enthusiastic songs—the same songs I had been singing for the past 5 years, and I knew them all! Then we heard some testimonies, and I really got excited because they were what Jesus had done TODAY. None of the old "saved and sanctified for 75 years bit," but fresh manna for the meeting.

We began to relax a little because the Spirit of the Lord was so real. Then as if on cue, with everyone being directed by God Himself, people began singing in a most unusual way. The only word we could distinguish, or thought we did, was the word "Hallelujah!" Other than that, it seemed like a beautiful harmonizing choir with about 1,000 voices humming. I looked at Charles and said, "What's that?" He looked back at me saying, "I don't know, what do you think it is?"

We were irresistibly drawn to this beautiful singing. It built up to a soft crescendo, and then just like it started, it stopped! Without being told, everyone seemed to know exactly when to stop. Spiritual goosepimples ran up and down our spines. It was the most beautiful singing we had ever heard. Willie Murphy afterwards announced, "For those of you not familiar with this type of singing, it is called 'singing in the Spirit.'"

It was beautiful, and never to be forgotten, because it was a miracle, a supernatural work of God. The message followed, and it was full of love, power and obviously directed by the Lord. So far there had been no rolling on the floor, nothing out of order, nothing much different from lots of services we had conducted ourselves except for the singing in the Spirit. We were prepared, though, because we knew "something" was bound to happen.

Willie Murphy, just glowing with the love of God then asked the entire congregation to stand and to make a little cup out of our hands as we sang the song, "Fill My Cup, Lord!" Charles looked at me and I looked at Charles and said, "Shall we, or shall we not?" After all, we didn't do things like this in our church. I'm sure our conversation and the looks which passed between the two of us were hysterical. After all, I've always been a super enthusiastic Christian, but this was just a little too much.

Why? Looking back, I know why. I was aware that there were many women there who had heard me speak during the past week at the Pittsburgh Christian Women's Clubs, and if I were to be totally honest right now, I'd have to admit I was afraid of what someone might think if they saw me lifting my hands in the air.

I want to tell you an interesting side issue of this, too. Because of my natural enthusiasm, I really like to participate in a church service, and for years every time we would sing a song such as "Oh, How I Love Jesus", I would have to lift my hand up in joyous agreement that I really did LOVE Jesus (but only one hand). The thought of raising *two* hands was TOO MUCH, especially where some people could see me.

The Spirit of the Lord had been so gloriously felt during the entire evening there wasn't anything else we could do except be a part of this beautiful worship time. We decided to go ahead and participate, but I said, "Let's do it behind the pew, so no one will see us." We actually bent over and behind the pew we made a little cup with our hands. The words of the song go, "Fill my cup, Lord; I lift it up Lord" and everybody lifted their hands up, symbolically lifting their cup to the Lord. . .

Do you know what Charles and I did without a word to each other? We both came out from behind the pew and lifted our cup to the Lord to be filled, and it was beautiful. The song went on, "Come and quench this thirsting of my soul; Bread of Heaven, Feed me 'til I want no more; Fill my cup, fill it up and make me whole." Who doesn't want to be filled up and have the thirsting of their soul quenched? Everyone who loves God wants this.

The song ended, and then they invited anyone who wanted to receive the baptism with the Holy Spirit to go through a side door. Charles and I looked at each other and the silent words we exchanged said, "That's not for us! Let's get out of here." In my mind I secretly wondered why they were ashamed to do whatever they had to do to you in public, instead of having to take you off to some dark corner. (Probably to hit you!)

We left, but the singing in the Spirit lingered on. We kept saying to each other, "How did they do that?" We tried to imitate the sound, but we couldn't do it. I believe when we heard the miracle of singing in the Spirit, this was the thing that made us believe that speaking in tongues was genuine and of God!

The next day was another never-to-be forgotten day. We had heard a lot about Kathryn Kuhlman and the divine healings that took place in her "miracle" services, but we had never attended one. The next morning there was to be one at the First Presbyterian Church, and a friend of ours volunteered to take us. We got there in plenty of time, but the crowd was so great, it was obvious that many were going to be shut out. We prayed fervently, asking God to let us get in, if He had a purpose in our being there, but if not, to let in the sick and afflicted. Just as the doors were beginning to close, we saw a little girl next to us who looked only a step away from death, and Charles and I both instinctively prayed, "God, if it's her or us, let her in, because she needs it more than we do!"

We stepped back to let her family ahead of us and then we heard an usher say, "Charles and Frances Hunter, will you step this way, please?" We could hardly believe our ears, but immediately stepped out and followed the usher to a seat in the second row. God wanted to be sure we could see everything clearly!

We watched things we had never seen before. We saw dramatic divine healings of all kinds—a deaf mute healed, the little girl we had prayed God would let in before us was healed, and we saw things first hand that we had heard about. When they came forward to testify of their healing, we noticed Kathryn Kuhlman just laid her hands on them and they all fell backwards. We had previously heard of this, and I felt it must be for weaklings or something. Either that, or she pushed them over! When I saw Kathryn Kuhlman for the first time, I realized she wasn't big enough to push anybody over, and yet here I was sitting in the second row and watching as many as 6 or 8 people all falling "under the power" at the same time. I couldn't understand it, but I still wondered if there wasn't some kind of a trick connected with it.

All of a sudden Kathryn left the podium and announced that the power of God was so strong He didn't need her there, so she said she was going to do something that she normally didn't do. She was going to walk down the center aisle, and she asked that no one touch her and she also asked that no one come out of their seat until she called them. She came down to the second row and turned to the seat across the aisle from where we were. She saw Ralph Wilkerson, pastor of the Melodyland Christian Center, and motioned for him to come out. He's bigger than she is, so I decided she couldn't very well push him over. She laid her hands on him and just said, "Jesus, bless him" and this big man fell over backwards. I looked at him real good, and he looked like he was enjoying whatever was going on. The ushers helped him to his feet, and again she laid her hands on him, and again, down he went! I couldn't believe my eyes, and then I looked directly at Kathryn, and saw she was pointing her long slender finger, and on the end of that finger was ME! I decided I was bigger than she was, so I stepped out. She just laid those soft hands on my temples ever so gently and asked God to bless me, and bless me He did, because would you like to guess where I was? Right on the floor! And in my best dress besides, knowing I had to speak at a luncheon that day! I could have cared less. I felt as if I was in heaven. The Spirit of God had breathed on me and I felt like a feather as I went down! I have never been the same!

On the way home from Pittsburgh, I opened my Bible to the 18th chapter of John and began reading, and you'd never guess what I discovered! An interesting verse that I knew God had just put in the Bible that very afternoon because I had never seen it before. Verses 4-6 read: "Jesus fully realized all that was going to happen to him. Stepping forward to meet them he asked, 'Whom are you looking for?' 'Jesus of Nazareth,' they replied. 'I am he,' Jesus said. And as He said it, THEY ALL FELL BACKWARDS TO THE GROUND!'" I almost tore Charles apart right on the plane yelling, "Look, look, look what it says in the Bible about falling under His power!" Once more God had let us see and taste of His supernatural power.

Go back with me a little bit, will you? I'd like to share how I happened to be speaking at the Holy Spirit Teaching Mission. I had received an invitation and was praising the Lord because the invitation happened to be on the day our daughter was to graduate from high school. I declined the invitation, feeling very happy because "I knew the Lord didn't want me involved with those charismatic people," but because God had begun drawing me to Him in another area of my life, I added a P.S. on the letter. "If you want me to speak there, and you can change the date, I'll be glad to come."

I mailed the letter. I never knew that mail could go so fast between Houston and Miami, because the next morning I had a telephone call from Miami asking me to choose what day I could come to speak at a luncheon. I knew I couldn't lie and tell them that I was going to be busy until Jesus came back, so I made another date with them.

The week after we returned from Pittsburgh, I flew to Miami completely bathed in prayer that "nothing bad would happen" while I was there. I was so concerned about being "beaten on the head" or something equally disastrous, I had called my beloved Miami pastor and asked him to round up some of my non-Pentecostal friends to go along with me and protect me from anything those "tongues" people might do to me.

I returned the same afternoon, but in that short space of time, God granted an experience I'll never forget. I was well aware of the fact that almost 100% of the charismatic group had received the baptism with the Holy Spirit. I was also aware of the fact that they were going to "pray tongues down on me" and I was also equally sure they weren't going to succeed. After lunch I again heard the singing of that heavenly choir where all the voices had been orchestrated by God Himself. "Singing in the Spirit" really united our hearts.

Then it was time for me to speak. So much prayer had gone up before my arrival that the day was beautiful beyond belief. The Spirit of the Lord was so strong, it was one of those special times when I felt I could actually reach out and physically touch the Holy Spirit, His presence was so real. As I closed in prayer, the Lord directed me to do something I normally never do. He directed me to give them a moment of silence to look at their own lives. In that moment of silence with the presence of God so real, someone quietly began to speak beautiful, loving, soothing words in a language I did not understand. It sounded like one or two sentences and that was all. I thought to myself, "That must be tongues, but it's beautiful!" Instantly there was an interpretation. "The words you have heard from the lips of Frances Hunter are not her words. They are Mine. Take heed and obey."

The Spirit of God crackled like electricity through the room.

No other words were spoken, but it was a moment of Eternity. No one could have been there and ever again doubted the reality of God. The tremendous love which filled the room was indescribable!

As my friends who had gone with me to "protect" me took me back to the airport to return to Texas, the fact that the Spirit of the Lord was upon all of us was apparent. One of them said, "You know, if I had to make a choice between being dried up or emotional, I'd pick being emotional. How about you?"

I had to honestly answer, "So would I," and with those words God tightened that gossamer web closer around me.

CHAPTER 5
THE "NO NO"
By Charles

"La, la, la, la, la, la, la, la! "

That was my first introduction to speaking in tongues, and that's as near as my father ever got to understanding the baptism with the Holy Spirit. If you could have heard how he said it, you would be quite sure he wanted no part of it. He felt this was the silliest, most useless, and wholly ungodly gibberish he had ever heard. He said the "tongues" people work themselves up into a false emotional high and artificially make utterances they create by their tongues going "la, la, la, la." Because we children never doubted Papa's wisdom, this became part of my "doctrine" and it lasted about forty years.

As I have searched for the source of the beliefs and opinions I held about tongues, I sent my mind hurling back through time, grasping the tiny pieces of recalled thoughts and pulling together the story that placed speaking in tongues in the "no-no" of my religious world. You will notice in the beginning part of this book Frances and I refer often to beliefs about "tongues". We had never associated this with the Holy Spirit. We did not understand that speaking in tongues had anything to do with the baptism with the Holy Spirit.

Because of our misunderstanding of the baptism, we are deliberately leaving in our reference to "tongues" as we relate our pre-baptism beliefs.

I can still hear Papa today. My first recollection of anything religious was when he and Mama became Christians when I was about eight years old. Although their formal education was very limited, their spiritual education was deep and strong. It came mostly from reading the Bible and just trusting God's Holy Spirit to teach them. They were two of the most beautiful, simple, child-like saints of God I have ever known and I was richly blessed under their parental instruction.

My mother is still alive at age 84 and her faith is as simple as the trust of a little girl, and so very, very great. Papa's attitudes were gentle and kind, molded in the loving likeness of Jesus. He was a strong disciplinarian, and the most severe discipline was that which he meted out to himself in his relentless search for God's plan for his life.

When I was twelve years old our family found the church denomination in which I was to worship for the next thirty-five years. It is a church that beautifully proclaims the truths of the teachings of Jesus and again I was blessed to be in such an atmosphere to learn. I became a Sunday School teacher in my teen years and wanted to be a good one for God. I diligently studied the Bible and my lessons, seeking all the knowledge I could find to do an outstand-

ing job. In the process of accumulating this knowledge, I became legalistic about many of my beliefs
and dogmatically insisted my beliefs were right, no
matter who challenged them.

The more I was challenged, the harder I studied
to be able to prove my beliefs, and probably even
harder to disprove my opponent's. What battles I
fought!

About this time I read how the chosen children
of Israel tried so hard to legalistically obey the once
simple laws of God. They made them so complex
and impossible by applying their own ideas and in-
terpretations. Yet I became just as legalistic in my
unbending opinions formed about many doctrines,
among which was the doctrine of "tongues". Most of
the children of Israel had their eyes so fixed on their
doctrines that they didn't see Jesus. I really believe I
had wandered into the same desert of defeat, as a
"Christian," as they had. The wall I built around my
doctrines was so solid that I, too, couldn't always see
Jesus.

How very simple are the teachings of Jesus
when we allow the Holy Spirit full control of our
minds and our desires, and just simply accept and
believe all He says.

One of my walls enclosed the belief that tongues
were humanly coerced upon others by "those Pentecostal people" and with all of *my* doctrinal wisdom I thought of this as a pathetic misapplication of
the Bible truths. I recall when I was about fourteen
years old, going to a Pentecostal tent meeting one
night. I was just a few seats away from the altar

where people gathered and knelt on the sawdust covered ground. A young girl, a little younger than I, was one of those at the altar. I was close enough that I could hear the instructions being given to her by the altar workers. There was a lot of urging about speaking in tongues and it really turned me off the *way* they did it. I heard them tell her to say "glory" and obediently she did. Then they said say "glory, glory," then, "glory, glory, glory" and they kept her repeating the word faster and faster and faster until it became a muddled garbling of sounds at which they victoriously shouted, "She's got it! She's got it!" I was filled with utter disgust. They may only have been awkward in their instructions, but it left me cold.

My mind was closed to tongues after that for a long, long time. Do you notice how we have the power to close our minds? And God does not compel us to open them to His bountiful ways. We will never be forced to take what we don't want, even if it is what God wants us to have. It's so easy to put *our* doctrines in front of God's doctrines and block our view of Jesus. It's never important at all what *we* think. It's so necessary to release our minds and hearts to the acceptance of God. He longs to tell us what He would like to give us. It's all in His Word. His gifts are so much better than the man-made beliefs which we are inclined to cling to so firmly.

In 1968 I totally released control of all of my life to God and asked Him with all the earnestness I possessed to take all of my life and make me spiritually what He wanted me to be. I simply turned loose.

When I was seventeen years old I was "saved". It was not until I was 48 that I finally wanted to yield everything to His control. I know now that this is the all-important start of being baptized with the Holy Spirit. We must first give up "self", then let that emptied temple, vacated of selfish purposes, be filled with God himself—filled with the Holy Spirit.

During the thirty-one years I spent in a spiritual desert of religious activities I set up defenses against attacks on my religion and my pride. I recall one time attempting to defend my beliefs to friends of another denomination and was embarrassed in my weakness but too proud to admit I failed. My opponent also failed, in my opinion, to prove his doctrine was better than mine. I was a man of strong determination so in my semi-shocked, embarrassed state I searched for a summary of the beliefs of my church. That was supposed to be what I believed, but since I wasn't sure how to define and support it to others I was not sure about what I was so sure about.

I found a little tract which really condensed it into about ten one-line facts. So, I memorized it— I put on what seemed to be the whole armor of my church (of course the Bible says the whole armor of God). Now I was fully fortified. Although it wasn't a part of the pamphlet, my first description of my church was "it is non-Pentecostal." Another denomination (Pentecostal) had the same name as mine and this was a constant source of embarrassment to me. But after surrendering myself utterly, there was nothing left of me to be embarrassed about.

Then, in the new spiritual world in which I began to live about three years ago, I began to face many issues honestly which had seemed so important doctrinally. As these were brought to my attention by the Holy Spirit, I would openly discuss them with God. I was finally willing to allow God, through His Word, to defend His own doctrines even if they differed from mine! Some of His teachings just didn't fit comfortably in my mind. And yet, because I gave Him all of me, I sincerely wanted Him to have His way even if it changed the way which I had presumed was His way. One of these controversial subjects was tongues. When I came upon scriptures about tongues I began discussing with God the meaning they might have in my life in just the same way that I was seeking His application of every scripture. I really sincerely wanted God to change anything He wanted to, no matter what it was.

I practically lived in the New Testament for over a year following my plea for God to take all of me. I felt the power of the Holy Spirit beginning to work in my life. He was softening my harsh attitudes. I was filled with a tremendous desire to do anything He wanted me to do, yielding moment by moment, thought by thought, to everything He was teaching me. I continued seeking more and more and more of Him; asking Him to control my every thought and looking for His desires in every word He spoke to me through the Bible, now made alive by the Holy Spirit controlling my life. NOTHING MATTERED TO ME EXCEPT TO DO ALL HE

WANTED. It was in this magnificent presence of God that He started softening the mortar in the walls which were so solidly set by years of hardening against this mysterious realm of the baptism of the Holy Spirit. This was just one of my structures He wanted to demolish so He could construct a more proper temple in which He could dwell; one in which He could freely move in all the areas, and not be shut out by the rooms *I* wanted to occupy and control. Prior to this my temple had no room for tongues.

God had moved me into another denomination for about two years. One of His purposes was to free me from my old church responsibilities and from the environment where I was content to live within doctrinal habits, in seclusion from the open freedom of the moving of the Holy Spirit. He wanted me to breathe fresh spiritual air and wanted to breathe into me a new life—His life, His Holy Spirit.

During this time God brought into my life a deeply spiritual man in whom I had great confidence. He discussed the baptism of the Holy Spirit and speaking in tongues as he shared his personal experience with me. One thing he said was completely new to me: that he could pray in tongues at any time he wanted to. This surprised but fascinated me. I guess I had presumed this was something that would come unexpectedly and to do uncontrollable things to you.

I was willing to breach all teachings of my life in this matter if God wanted me to do so. My beliefs and pride vanished and I was ready to accept anything from God, even tongues!

CHAPTER 6

THEN IT HAPPENED!
By Frances

January of 1971 found us in Hawaii, and the Lord really granted a harvest out there—not only in souls for His kingdom, but a harvest of Christian fellowship. Our Hawaiian friends, the McCulloughs, gave me two books called *"Crisis-America"* and *"You Shall Receive. . ."* by George Otis. I read *"Crisis-America"* which I thought was excellent, but the other one smacked of "tongues", and I almost threw it away as I had done all other books of this nature, but I didn't. Somehow God's Holy Spirit impressed me to keep the book, so I stuck it in my luggage and thought maybe I'd read it "some time" after I got home . . . but I didn't! I hid it! I didn't want anyone to find that kind of literature in my house.

Came the summer of 1971 and Charles and I went to the International Christian Booksellers Convention in Denver. We were at the booth where MY LOVE AFFAIR WITH CHARLES was being featured, just looking the situation over prior to our autographing session. As we looked around the huge convention hall, we saw directly across the aisle from us a sign which said "George Otis autographing here from two to four p.m." Then I saw a very distinguished man sitting there autographing books, and I thought, "I wonder who that is." Then another thought came to my mind and I said to Charles, "Who is George Otis?" A little bell had begun to ring in my mind concerning that name and I was trying to recall what it was.

Then it dawned on me! I said, "Charles, that's GEORGE OTIS!" I grabbed Charles and ran over to meet him. I remembered that this man had a tremendous influence in the life of Pat and Shirley Boone. He's in their book. We had just heard a lot about him in Hawaii. Then it came back—this was the man who had written *"You Shall Receive. . ."* (which I hadn't read) and others. The Lord must have shoved us across that aisle, because we had an uncontrollable urge to meet George Otis.

We introduced ourselves, and I said, "You don't know who we are, but that's all right, because we know who you are." George Otis came back with the most shocking statement I could imagine because he said, "Are you really Frances Hunter? I just got back from Hawaii and everywhere I went all I heard about was the way you turned that island upside down for Christ."

I was flabbergasted that anyone like him would have ever heard of me. I couldn't believe my ears, but I could believe the love of God which radiated from him. We talked and talked and our spirits blended beautifully with his as we shared what the Lord had been doing in our lives. Never was there a moment of strangeness as we talked—but then, in

Christ there never is, is there? Later in the afternoon, Pat and Shirley Boone came over and we had a marvelous time praying with them as we knelt on the floor of the Convention Hall in Denver.

Then God had us do an unusual thing. We sought out George Otis again and said to him, "If you're ever in the Houston area, we'd love to have you stay in our 'guest room for the Lord.'" The only other ones we extended an invitation to were Pat and Shirley. We are gone so much of the time we don't often extend invitations because we know we won't be there, but we especially went out of our way to invite George.

In August I went to the hospital for eye surgery and the way the Lord guided my recovery was fabulous. Even so, there is still a certain amount of weakness after an operation. The day after I came home from the hospital I got a telephone call from California. It was George Otis' secretary who said, "George asked me to call you and tell you he'd love to accept your invitation to stay at your house. He'll be arriving too early that first Saturday morning. He will stay in a motel that night. You can contact him at the Full Gospel Businessmen's meeting and he'll go home with you and stay with you Saturday night if it is convenient for you."

We hadn't even invited George for that weekend, but I didn't think too much about it because we had given him a "vague" invitation at the Christian Booksellers Convention, but I didn't realize the tremendousness of God's miracle until months later. Friends of George's had seen in the newspaper that he was coming to Houston and had called California asking him to stay with them, but God's Holy Spirit crossed the communication lines and the call was placed to us, accepting the "wrong" invitation. WOW! Praise God!

I immediately started to tell her that while we would sincerely love to have him, I had just gotten home from the hospital and it would be impossible for me to have a guest at this time. Those words didn't come out of my mouth at all! What did come out really shocked me because I said, "We'd love to have him to be our guest. We'll pick him up Saturday at the meeting."

I listened to her further instructions and hung up the telephone and almost collapsed. This was ridiculous except I knew it had to be of the Lord. Humanly there was no way I would be physically ready to have a guest in just one more day. I WENT TO BED! Before I did, however, I prayed and said, "Lord, you'll have to give me the strength I need, because I'll never be able to do it."

Then I picked up the phone by the side of my bed and called Charles and said, "Honey, do you know what I just did?" And then I told him. Charles is so protective where I'm concerned that I knew he'd call George's office right back and tell them I wasn't able to have company, BUT HE DIDN'T. He said in his real sweet way, "Honey, I'm sure the Lord will give you just exactly the strength you'll need while George is here."

I fell back in bed exhausted! Then I remembered I hadn't read George's book and I thought it would be awful if I hadn't read my guest's book. I scrambled out of bed, praying all the time, "God, where did I hide that book I didn't want anyone to see in this house?" Praise the Lord He had seen where I hid it and reminded me quickly where it was. I got as far as 18 pages then I just collapsed and went to sleep. The minute I awoke, however, I picked up the book again and read the balance of it, and somehow I KNEW then what was going to happen.

Charles and I talked late into the night about the genuineness of the gift of tongues and held to our "amended" opinion that it was genuine. It was scriptural, but it "might not" be for us. However, both of us prayed fervently that night and said, "Lord, if this is of You, let our minds be open and receptive to whatever You have for us."

The second morning after the telephone call, we were up at the crack of dawn, and left to go to the Full Gospel Businessmen's meeting to pick up George. We felt obligated to go because we didn't feel it would be polite not to attend the meeting where George was speaking, and we didn't think it would show much Christian love on our part if we came after the meeting. George later said he never dreamed we would attend the meeting, but there we were!

Later George said it really made him self-conscious when he knew we were present during the service in which he was speaking. He was afraid it might destroy our friendship since he thought we were against the baptism with the Holy Spirit. What he didn't know was how well the Holy Spirit had prepared us for the meeting God Himself arranged. We have often remembered this as we have hesitated in speaking to others about the baptism. Sometimes we forget that God has already gone ahead of us.

We were fascinated with George's testimony that day, seeing how God had worked in his life. The power and authority in his life were evident and his love for the Lord blazed!

The Jesus in Charles and me loved the Jesus in George!

After the meeting George held a session for those who were seeking the baptism with the Holy Spirit. Charles and I didn't want to go (I wonder if it was because we thought someone might see us?) but we wanted to be close enough to hear what was going on, but not close enough to get involved. Several people came to talk with us afterwards, so try as we might, we couldn't hear anything George said. We kept "stretching" our ears trying to hear what was going on, but couldn't hear a word. I whispered to Charles, "See, the Lord just doesn't want us to get involved with this kind of stuff!"

We had lunch with George and his Houston friends.

A question one friend asked me was, "How come George is staying with you when we asked him to stay with us?" I thought nothing of this until later when George realized God had purposely confused the telephone calls.

George came back to our house and we talked

about nothing but Jesus the entire time. Then we learned George was speaking again that night at the University of Houston. We sat right in the front, anticipating where he would put the people who came seeking the baptism. We wanted to be close enough to hear this time! We were eager to find out what was going on!

God had other plans! We thrilled again to George's message and when this meeting was over, we knew we would be in a good position to hear what was going on in the second meeting without getting involved. Then someone came and asked us to   Two or three times during George's teaching session on the Holy Spirit we tried to slip forward, but each time we got held up by someone else. We came home and all we talked about was Jesus, Jesus, Jesus! George had never yet even mentioned the baptism. He was just bubbling over with what God was doing in these days! As soon as we got in bed, we whispered to each other, "See, God doesn't want us involved because did you notice how He blocked us again from hearing what George said?"

But the Holy Spirit was still working, so we said, "But if You want to give it to us, just give it to us!" We laid there with our arms folded. NOTHING HAPPENED!

We got up the next morning to take George to a church where he was speaking. Our breakfast conversation was fabulous! Notice how God did the job as He always does, covered with His love. God knew our greatest dislike was people who had tried to cram "tongues" down our throat, but here we were with this fabulous guest in our home, and he hadn't yet said one word to us about the baptism. All we were talking about was the current miracles of Jesus.

Finally, I couldn't stand it any more. Here we had this man in our house, one who had written books about the ministry of the Holy Spirit, and he hadn't said a single solitary word to us! Finally *I* started the conversation and said: "George, you KNOW we don't speak in tongues, don't you?" (I'm sure I must have sounded real smug!) George said one of the funniest things I ever heard because he answered: "No, I hadn't noticed!" He went right on eating his breakfast. He didn't continue the conversation. So I did! I said, "We believe there is a genuine gift of tongues. There was a time we told God we didn't want it, but we realized how wrong this was, so we've told God if He wants to give it to us, we'll just take it. But we're not going to go out of our way to get it, because we just don't think we need it."

Now look at old self-righteous Frances, because I added: "The Bible says 'ye shall receive power', and you can look at our lives and see that God has already given us power." In love George said to me, "I know the power you've got in your life, because I've seen the evidence of what happened while you were in Hawaii, but wouldn't you like to have MORE power from God?"

I honestly felt like I'd been kicked right in the stomach! Who was I to tell God I had so much power I didn't need any more? I felt a little sick. I shot up a silent prayer to God apologizing for thinking that I didn't need any more power than He had already given me.

Then George made a challenging statement, "Frances, you've already got ONE Hot Line to Heaven. Wouldn't you like to have TWO?" (He was referring to one in English, and one in the spirit—the natural and the supernatural!)

Again that sickening feeling in the pit of my stomach! Why shouldn't I want a second Hot Line to Heaven? Why shouldn't I want a "double-portion?" Then I began to use the usual cliches I had heard so many times, "Well, then, just let Him give it to me." George came back with, "God doesn't work that way. He won't force the baptism on you any more than He will force salvation on anyone. YOU have to take the first step, then God will do the rest."

Then Charles said, "Maybe God is building a reputation for us as we share across the nation to show you can be filled with the Holy Spirit without speaking in tongues." George looked up from his breakfast and again in great love said, "Jesus worked without reputation," and another fetter broke which bound "self-righteous" Charles. (That's what Charles called himself).

By this time, breakfast was almost over and we had to race to get dressed for the service where George was to speak. As we were walking to get into the car, I panicked because I realized that George wouldn't be back to our house before returning to California. We were to take him right to the airport after church, and we still didn't understand this "tongues" business. I hadn't forgotten the two kicks that George had given me, so as we stood at the door the words just tumbled out of my mouth: "You don't by any chance have a tape or something we could listen to, do you?" George said, "I just happen to have one in my suitcase, and I'll consider it a privilege to leave it with you."

George had one unedited tape which he had felt impressed to finish just before he came to Houston—the first and only one he had ever made (at that time) teaching on the baptism with the Holy Spirit. I believe God's Holy Spirit had George record it just for us! George gave us the tape HOW TO RECEIVE THE GIFT OF THE HOLY SPIRIT that was to dramatically change our lives and complete the gossamer web that God had been spinning for years around us.

I couldn't wait to get home from the airport. I was completely exhausted by this time, so I fell in bed and suggested we play the tape. Charles, in his beautiful wisdom, knew I'd never be able to listen because I was so tired. He said he thought we'd better wait until the next night when I wasn't quite so exhausted.

I could hardly wait until Charles got home on Monday night! I had reread everything I could find on the subject of tongues all day Monday. I had searched the Scriptures, asking God to reveal the truth to me as to what He wanted in this area of my life. And all of a sudden certain portions of the Bible took on a new and greater meaning. I read and reread the book of Acts that day, and when I read Acts

10:44: "Even as Peter was saying these things, the Holy Spirit fell upon all those listening! The Jews who came with Peter were amazed that the gift of the Holy Spirit would be given to Gentiles too! *But there could be no doubt about it, for they heard them speaking in tongues and praising God."* (God! When did you put that new verse in the Bible?)

A thought came into my mind . . . How could they KNOW the Gentiles were filled with the Holy Spirit? The last sentence really hit me, "for they heard them speaking in tongues and praising God." Was this the sign, then? Was this an automatic overflow? Was this for ALL believers? I continued reading and came to Acts 11:15: "Well, I began telling them the Good News, but just as I was getting started with my sermon, the Holy Spirit fell on them, JUST AS HE FELL ON US AT THE BEGINNING."

How did Paul KNOW the Holy Spirit fell on them? Did they immediately begin to manifest the fruit of the Spirit? How could they in such a short time? They couldn't, so all of a sudden I began to wonder if, when the Bible says, "the Holy Spirit fell on them, just as He fell on us at the beginning," it meant the same sign, speaking in tongues! I went back to Acts 2:4: "and *everyone* present was filled with the Holy Spirit and began speaking in languages they didn't know, for the Holy Spirit gave them this ability." Was this a manifestation of the enduement with power from on high? I began to wonder...

Then I read I Cor. 14:4-5 and it said, "He that

speaketh in an UNKNOWN tongue edifieth himself; but he that prophesieth edifieth the church." I had always misunderstood the word "edifieth" and took it to mean "glorifieth" himself (and I didn't think that was good), but I took time out to look it up in the dictionary and it said "build up one's faith." And I thought, "So what's wrong with building up your own faith. NOTHING!" I read I Cor. 14:19 which I had heard so many times, "yet in the church I had rather speak FIVE words with my understanding that by my voice I might teach others also, then ten thousand words in an UNKNOWN tongue." (KJV)

Always I had heard this comment on that verse: "See even Paul said it was ridiculous to waste your time speaking in tongues, because five words in your own language are better than ten thousand in an unknown language." And he was right, but he said IN THE CHURCH. He didn't say anything in that verse about the privacy of your own prayer closet. I had always heard that verse used as one of the strongest arguments AGAINST tongues, but all of a sudden it began to speak to me in a totally different way.

I saw there were two kinds of tongues! One for public use which is one of the nine gifts of the Holy Spirit. The other for your private prayer life. The Bible didn't say to me any longer that tongues were wrong, but that there was a place for them, and a time for them, and a need for them to be in complete harmony with God's plan for our lives. I backed up and read some more.

I started at I Cor. 12 and read it over and over. I

got out the New English Bible, the Living Bible, the American Standard, the Revised Standard, the King James, every translation that I knew of and they all said about the same thing!

I quote from the New English Bible: "There are varieties of gifts, but the same spirit. There are varieties of service, but the same Lord. There are many forms of work, but all of them, in all men, are the work of the same God In each of us, the Spirit is manifested in one particular way, for some useful purpose." Listen to the Living Bible: "Now God gives us many kinds of special abilities, but it is the same Holy Spirit who is the source of them all. There are different kinds of service to God, but it is the same Lord as we are serving. There are many ways in which God works in our lives, but it is the same God who does the work in and through all of us who are His."

Suddenly I "grew up" enough to understand that God had NEVER said that we were all going to have the same abilities. God had never said He would treat each one of us exactly alike. God had never said we would all serve Him in exactly the same manner. He *did* say there were all kinds of gifts, and all kinds of services, but it is still the same God who does the different work in and through all of us who are His. I read every translation in our house, and they all included the same message. When they got to the 28th verse and listed the gifts of the Spirit, every version included the gift of speaking in tongues. Some refer to it as "ecstatic utterances," or "languages they have never learned"

have the same abilities. God had never said He
REFER TO IT. There isn't a single translation of the
Bible which leaves out this gift. Every translation
includes the gift of tongues along with all the other
gifts. Why, then, do we act like God made a mistake
when He included this gift right along with the eight
others? The Bible seals the fact that it IS a gift of the
same Holy Spirit who gives all the other gifts.
Wouldn't we have to deny all of them as relevant for
today if we deny one?

Well, then, how about the fact that it is listed
last? When Paul said, "covet earnestly the best
gifts," doesn't this mean we should covet those
listed first? Does Paul indicate anywhere which is
the most important of the gifts? Frankly, I would
like even the least of one of God's gifts, wouldn't
you? He does say, however, that even if you speak
with the tongues of men (your own mother tongue)
and of angels (your heavenly language) but have not
love, you are a real NOTHING! It doesn't say the
GIFT is a real nothing. It says YOU are a real
nothing if you exercise the gifts of the Spirit without
love. I again remembered all the arguments I had
heard about the gift of tongues being last, and that
being the reason we shouldn't seek that one. Paul
said seek ALL of them, and at one time or another,
we read of each of them working in Paul's life.

My thinking was changing—rapidly! I thought
of the years when I had said, "God, I DON'T want
that gift. That's no good!" Then I remembered that
for years I had said, "Well, God, if you want to give it
to me, that's O.K." Then I thought about what He

was saying to me today. He was saying, "You've sought all the others, why not this one?"

With that the last of my defenses folded, but I was still confused because I didn't realize that what I was seeking was the gift of the Holy Spirit, not the "gift" of tongues.

We bolted our supper down that Monday night and finished up quickly anything in the house that had to be taken care of. Then we hurried to bed, turned on the "TAPE" and listened. Before we listened, however, we prayed fervently, asking God to do what He wanted to do with our lives. We prayed, "God, if this is a new dimension You want in our lives, then let us be willing to take the first step and boldly ask for it."

Neither of us said a word until the end of the tape. We had listened very intently. We heard teaching from the Word that really made sense. We realized that in accepting the gift of salvation, each of us must take the first step, and then God will take the rest. We had to cry out to God for forgiveness of our sins and ask Jesus to come into our hearts before He gave us the gift of salvation. He did not make either of us accept it until we asked for it. And we said, "It's the same with the baptism—we have to take the first step."

We were especially impressed with one point. Remember Peter when he walked on the water? Peter himself had to put his foot over the side of the boat, and only then did Jesus make the water hard— hard enough for him to walk on. When Peter not only trusted Jesus' word to "Come! " but *acted* on it, the miracle happened.

We listened intently as the tape gave the instructions—nearly all of it scripture, and yet mentioning the fact that as intellectual adults we might feel foolish. But God puts a premium on obedience and coming as a little child. We played the tape again, and again we listened to the instructions which said to pray for Jesus to baptize with the Holy Spirit and then begin to speak as the Spirit gives the utterance.

George had suggested that we raise our hands in worship and surrender to God. There we lay, side by side, hands raised in worship to God. When the tape said, "NOW," the silence was deafening. You couldn't even hear either of us breathing. NOT A SINGLE SOLITARY SOUND CAME OUT OF EITHER ONE OF US! I couldn't have uttered a sound for anything! I looked at Charles and said, "Honey, why didn't you say something?" Charles looked back at me and with his fabulous dry sense of humor, he said, "Honey, George said to not think, but just to let sounds come out, and I can't make a sound without thinking, so I didn't do a thing!"

We decided we needed to listen to part of the tape again, so we did, and when we came to the part when George said, "NOW," we both raised our hands above our heads, looked at each other, and began laughing like a couple of idiots. I don't believe I ever felt so ridiculous in my entire life. I didn't know that I could be self-conscious around my beloved husband, but I was. We decided the Lord didn't want us to try this together, so we turned off the tape recorder and went to sleep.

I couldn't wait for Charles to go to work the next morning! Usually I kiss him "3,000" times before he goes to work and I'm still hanging on to him because I hate to let him go, but this morning I was practically shoving him out the door. The minute I heard his car go around the house, I ran for the bedroom. I didn't even take the breakfast dishes off the table. The Holy Spirit was really quickening my heart and I jumped back into bed and turned on the tape recorder. The thing that really stood out in my mind was how Jesus had made the water hard under Peter's feet.

Alone now, I listened to the tape all the way to the part where George said NOW! Then I turned off the tape recorder. There was no one in the room but Jesus and me, but the power and presence of God was as real as it had ever been in my life. I softly whispered a very simple little prayer, "God, if it's genuine, if it's real, if it's of You, and it's for me, then make the water hard, or in my case, make the air solid under the sound of my voice, and Jesus, I ask You to baptize me with the Holy Spirit."

In that moment of yielding to God of my mind, my soul, my spirit, my tongue, my brain, I gave just one or two little sounds, and instantly I was baptized with the Holy Spirit. The room was filled with the most beautiful glow you could ever imagine. I had to close my eyes! The splendor of the Lord was there! The entire room seemed bathed with the love of God. I thought surely I must be in heaven. Never have I felt such a helplessness before God as I did in that moment of yielding. Gone were the barriers I had built up ever since I became a Christian about the matter of praying in tongues. Out of my own mouth flowed the most beautiful, soft "love" language in the world. I knew I was praising and loving God just like the 120 did on the day of Pentecost.

I have never felt closer to God, more loved by God, more protected by Him, more sheltered by Him, or more full of love and praise for Him than in those moments. My cup was running over! I couldn't understand a word I was saying, but I knew God could. My heart knew that in my overflowing with love for the One who had so changed my life, I was praising His Holy Name, and I wasn't cluttering up the praise with some of my own inadequate words, but was using the special "love" language which He had given to me. Jesus speaking of this had said, "Out of your innermost being shall flow rivers of living waters."

I could have kept praying all day, it was so glorious! But the Lord reminded me of the one whom He had joined with me to become one, so I quickly called Charles. All I said was, "Honey, it's true! There IS a beautiful heavenly language and I've got it!"

Then I began to cry. (Praise the Lord and pass the Kleenex). . .

Then Charles began to cry (Praise God for his tender heart) as he said, "Let me hear you."

At that time I believed I had to have my hands over my head to speak in tongues; and since I was holding the telephone, I told him it was impossible.

Charles said, "Please try, honey!" So I "scooched" down in bed again, trying to hold the decorator phone on my shoulder, and still keep my hands up in the air!

I hadn't forgotten! Over the telephone I prayed for Charles. All he could say was, "It's beautiful, honey, it's beautiful," as the power of God melted the telephone wires with love. I told Charles the one thing that had helped me so much was asking Jesus to make the air hard.

Then I prayed, "Lord, so that we will stay on the same spiritual level, I'm going to ask that you baptize Charles with the Holy Spirit and give him a heavenly language in the car on the way home tonight."

It was a blessed day! I prayed in English! I prayed in tongues! I praised God in English! I praised God in tongues! I sang in English! I sang in the Spirit!

The glory of the Lord never left our house that day! I had gone to the store when Charles came home and for once he was glad I wasn't there. (He wanted to pray alone.) When Joan and I later drove in the driveway, Charles raced out to meet us and I knew by the expression on his face what had happened. God had answered our prayer! He didn't even wait for me to ask the question, because he knew I was going to ask, "Did you receive your special language?" He simply said, "I did!"

Then it was my turn to cry! I had asked God to bless Charles the same day, and He did! What rejoicing! What wild joy! What love of God! (Now many don't have the same emotional reaction that we did at the moment of receiving the Holy Spirit. Remember it isn't a matter of feeling, but obedience that counts.)

God had woven the final gossamer thread, but it didn't turn out to be a web at all. It turned out to be the lovely bow on another of the beautiful gifts just for us—this time the REAL gift accompanied by a special "prayer" language to be used for Him and for His purpose. . .

Charles

Yielding myself to what God wants has been one of the most exciting, most marvelous thrills of my new life. Jesus yielded His desires so completely to those of His Father that I didn't know what He wanted. Probably the biggest reason I didn't know was that I was trying to serve Him on a part-way basis. He made His commands very clear to the Is-raelites, but they found other desires greater than obedience to Him. It was the law, and not love, which motivated them.

As a carnal Christian I used to try to obey the law which really was more the law of my own church. My church law said speaking in tongues was a "no-no" and the teachings of man molded my at-titude. The Holy Spirit was now absorbing my every thought and desire but I was suspicious and doubt-ful about this gift so clearly offered in the New Tes-tament. I was hesitant to venture away from the safe harbor of my teachings—my church law.

For a time I was attending another church

which did not even teach the simplicity of salvation: asking God to forgive our sins and asking Jesus to come into our lives and control our desires and thoughts. One Sunday the minister, whom I love very much, began his sermon by saying, "I don't care what 'they' say, I'm going to preach this sermon." He then preached the beautiful plan of salvation for which Jesus gave His life. For one day he risked the security of being controlled by the rules of his church, which was the same undemolished wall that stood between me and the acceptance of one of God's beautiful gifts—the wall within which denominations so often theologically enslave their people from the freedom He wants to give. The absence of my willingness to relinquish a man-taught doctrine in favor of seeking the instructions of the Holy Spirit through the truths of the Bible was a wall which stood between me and the gift. We can never know the meaning of the truths of the Bible when we refuse to seek His desires. We only know God's promises *after* we, by faith, obey what He says. We must take the first step.

Frances and I share all our thoughts with each other and because our thoughts are constantly about God and Christ Jesus we seek together to know everything we can of His instructions. This we were doing one day as we flew from the Pacific Northwest to Los Angeles. We really began discussing with God and each other about whether tongues was to be a part of our lives. We doubted they would be and in this way we sort of doubted God's Word. Our usual reply to questions concerning this was that we were willing to have this gift but that God apparently had other plans for us.

Then we read the book A NEW SONG by Pat Boone. We were made aware of the beauty and genuineness of this gift. It was not referred to by this disturbing word "TONGUES," but was described as the heavenly language of love as Shirley, Pat and their daughters each were given their own individual praise language to be used just for their personal private talking to God. Someway, I knew there was more to what happened to them than just a "thing" called speaking in tongues. My heart melted in this pool of love.

Since Frances has told you about our encounter with George Otis and his visit in our home, I will just mention some of the other advances the Holy Spirit made through him in my life. Because we were well aware that George spoke in tongues, and because we knew very clearly that his visit with us was planned and timed perfectly by God, we were eagerly anticipating his arrival. When we heard George's testimony and felt the power of the Holy Spirit in him, our confidence in his relationship to God was complete. The love, joy, peace, gentleness and a bushel of the other fruit of the Spirit radiated abundantly from him.

George became the channel of God's plan in our lives as the Holy Spirit through him completely prepared our hearts and minds. In the informality of our breakfast room even as we began discussing the subject of tongues I believe the Holy Spirit had already fully won the doctrinal battle and had given us a wholehearted desire for this gift.

Two days later my heart leaped with excitement as Frances shared with me the beautiful new language God had bestowed upon her only minutes before. Tears of joy filled my eyes as this beautiful language flowed from her lips. I didn't understand the words but my spirit understood their significance.

God is so thoughtful and considerate! That whole day I was working at the side of at least one other person, but for the few moments Frances was on the phone with me everyone left the room. God gave me the privacy to feel the new depth of His love in Frances and the fresh fragrance of the Holy Spirit as she shared her new language with me.

After Frances called that morning I could hardly keep from bubbling over with excitement, thrill and almost uncontrollable eagerness to get through my day and be free to accept the gift I was certain God had for me. I was working in downtown Houston that day and as soon as the work day ended, I rushed to the car, and moved into the heavy traffic. I had been praising God all day (I have learned to "think to God" as I work) and now I was asking Him to prepare me for receiving the gift as soon as I reached the freeway.

I get excited when I have a special gift for Frances or Joanie. I can hardly wait to give it to them. He wants so much to give us His abundance, I'm sure He was as excited as I.

He seemed to move cars out of my way to rush me onto the freeway. Just as soon as I rounded the curve which leads onto the freeway, I prayed, "Jesus, I ask you to baptize me with the Holy Spirit and give me a heavenly language as you did Frances."

If you think Frances had a problem raising her hands, trying to balance the telephone on her shoulder while lying down, you should have seen me! I was driving 60 miles an hour in freeway traffic. (You don't really have to raise your hands. It is necessary to raise your heart in love and praise to God, to keep your spiritual eyes on Jesus lest you sink back into self as Peter did.) I simply opened my mouth, making only one or two sounds. Out of my mouth poured a beautiful, new, wonderful heavenly language of love, unbelievable and gloriously genuine! The car was flooded with the glory of God as I yielded my deepest desires to Him in a new-found release. What magnificent and overwhelming joy I experienced as I felt the very presence of Jesus as the Holy Spirit within me was speaking with my mouth, my voice, my tongue directly to my Father in heaven. Jesus said He provided for us to go into the very presence of God Himself. At that moment I felt I had literally done so. Never before had I felt so completely under the power of the Holy Spirit or so released to His Control. This mighty miracle of streams of living sounds flowed out of my mouth as the Holy Spirit spoke without the direction of my human mind. Just as I had released my life to Him, so I had now released my tongue. The Holy Spirit confirmed His control of my life, my mind, my desires, my spirit, as He physically assumed control over my tongue. Hallelujah! The "heavenly language" continued to flood my soul all the way home for the next twenty minutes.

For the only time in our married life, I prayed Frances and Joanie would not be home because I just wanted to submerge into this presence of God. Again His love blessed as I rushed into our study, sat in my chair at my desk, and raised *both* arms as far toward heaven as I could. The joy of the Lord came upon me as I praised Him in my beautiful language of love for thirty wonderful minutes. Then I heard our car come into the driveway, and ran with out-stretched arms to my sweetheart. In bursting joy I simply said, "I did!" How we thanked Jesus for baptizing us with the Holy Spirit and bestowing upon both of us in the same day our heavenly praise language!

CHAPTER 7
THERE IS A DIFFERENCE

One of the biggest surprises came when we realized there was a difference between the "gift of tongues" and the "prayer" tongues. George had shown us this from the Scriptures. This really helped clear up some of the confusion. We had always put them all into one category, that of "speaking in tongues" and NEVER realized any difference at all, nor did we associate this with the power of the Holy Spirit. No wonder we thought, "Do all speak in tongues?" applied to us negatively.

Praise God for His grace because we are beginning to be aware more and more of the complete misunderstanding that exists concerning the outward sign of having been baptized with the Holy Spirit. Many people who praise God in their own private language have never received the "gift" of tongues to the assembly, and many never will.

Look what the Bible says: "Seven weeks had gone by since Jesus' death and resurrection, and the Day of Pentecost had now arrived. As the believers met together that day, suddenly there was a sound like the roaring of a mighty windstorm in the skies above them and it filled the house where they were meeting. Then what looked like flames or tongues of fire appeared and settled on their heads. And *everyone* present was filled with the Holy Spirit and began speaking in languages they didn't know, for the Holy Spirit gave them this ability" (Acts 2:1-4).

The Bible specifically says "all" or "everyone" was filled with the Holy Spirit. It doesn't say part, it doesn't say just some, it says "everyone". Every person who was gathered in the upper room was of one accord. They wanted to be obedient. They didn't want to miss out on anything! They were excited! Jesus had promised them power from on high! They had gone to wait, as Jesus told them, until the Holy Spirit came after He had returned to His Father. These were not casual Christians!

Can you imagine the air of excitement that must have filled the upper room? Can you imagine the suspense of wondering about the exact moment when the Holy Spirit would arrive? They were all anticipating something they didn't know anything about. Can't you just hear some of the conversations going on between Peter and James and John? "How's He going to do this? What will the Comforter be like? And how is He going to give us power in our lives? Will we feel anything? Will we be able to see the Holy Spirit? Will it hurt? Will we be frightened?

Can you imagine James saying, "Peter, why don't you go check on your boat? Are you sure it was anchored good?" More than that, can you imagine Peter's reply: "James, you're out of your mind. Jesus told us to wait in the upper room and if you think I'm going to take a chance on missing out on this, you'd better think again."

They wanted to be right where Jesus had told them to be when the promised Holy Spirit (or Comforter) came. They weren't there grumbling, they were there *expecting!* Expecting the gift which was to give them power to be witnesses in "Jerusalem, throughout Judea, in Samaria and to the ends of the earth, about the death and resurrection of Jesus." They were ALL expecting, and not one of them was disappointed, because the gift of the Holy Spirit was for every single one of them. Notice that every translation says that they immediately began speaking in languages they didn't know.

How could they possibly speak all these different languages they never knew? "For the Holy Spirit gave them this ability." It was the Holy Spirit who had now come to empower the believer who gave them this ability. They could never have done it on their own. And it is the same Holy Spirit who comes to empower the believer today and give them this same ability.

Jesus Christ is the same yesterday, today and forever!

As Peter continued with this magnificent sermon that day, he said: "And now He sits on the throne of the highest honor in heaven, next to God. And just as promised, the Father gave Him the authority to send the Holy Spirit—with the results you are seeing and hearing today" (Acts 2:33).

As I reread this, how could they possibly *hear* unless there was an audible manifestation which accompanied the baptism of the Holy Spirit? The same thing is true today. Just as the Father gave Jesus the authority to send the Holy Spirit, He never withdrew this authority so the Holy Spirit is here today, FOR EVERY BELIEVER!

Again, "And Peter replied, 'Each one of you must turn from sin, return to God, and be baptized in the name of Jesus Christ for the forgiveness of your sins; then you also shall receive this gift, the Holy Spirit. For Christ promised him to *each* of you who has been called by the Lord our God, and to your children, and even to those in distant lands!'" (Acts 2:38-39).

"But the manifestation of the Spirit is given to *every* man to profit withal" (I Cor. 12:7 KJV). Therefore, the gift of the Holy Spirit, and the private "praise" language which is an overflowing, or manifestation of the Holy Spirit, is available to all. This is the Holy Spirit within us, making intercession for us in words we cannot understand. This is an earthward to heavenward praise and prayer language. This is the cry of the Holy Spirit from our innermost being speaking to the Father in Heaven concerning those needs for which we don't even know how to pray.

Now let's look at the "gift" of tongues. In I Corinthians, Chapter 12, we have an entire chapter devoted to the nine gifts of the Spirit. The "gifts" might also be called "jobs" or "abilities." To some individuals he has given the job of being an "apostle, a prophet, a teacher, an individual who performs miracles, a person who has the gift of healing, those who can help others, those who can get others to work together, and those who speak in languages they have never learned" (I Cor. 12:28).

The last one listed is the "gift" or "job" or "ability" to receive a message from God and then transmit it to an assembly out loud in a tongue to the group of believers. This type of tongue is to be followed by its companion gift of interpretation.

"Well, my brothers, let's add up what I am saying. When you meet together some will sing, another will teach, or tell some special information God has given him, or speak in an unknown language, or tell what someone else is saying who is speaking in the unknown language, but everything that is done must be useful to all, and build them up in the Lord. No more than two or three should speak in an unknown language, and they must speak one at a time, and someone must be ready to interpret what they are saying" (I Cor. 14:26-27).

Compare the difference between the "praise and prayer" tongue that is for all, and the tongues to the assembly that is not for all. When the anointing falls upon a person with a message FROM God, it is a message heaven to earth. This is a message from God to His people and in order for the congregation to understand it, it must be followed by an interpretation into the language they understand. The person who has the "gift" or "job" of interpretation has another gift to be manifested in partnership with the tongues spoken out. He receives the interpretation from God and transmits it to the congregation in their local language.

Now think back on what the "praise" tongue is.

It is just the reverse of the "public" tongue. It does not need an interpretation, because it is a prayer of intercession by the Holy Spirit directly to God. He is all Wisdom and all Knowledge. He understands all languages, so does not need anyone to interpret for Him. The prayer is to Him, and Him alone, and not to be shared with anyone on the earth. Remember this is the "earth to heaven" conversation. The other is a "heaven to earth" conversation, and there is a difference!

CHAPTER 8
TO HAVE AND HAVE NOT. . .

One of the questions that arose in my mind over the years actually had a very simple answer. The only problem was my own lack of understanding. At various times we all have a tendency to put our eyes on people instead of on Christ. God had a big lesson for me to learn in this area concerning the subject of tongues.

I had seen people who professed to know the "fullness of the Spirit" because they spoke in tongues, but whose personal lives certainly didn't in any way evidence a godly life. And I was confused. Probably one of the most persistent people who insisted I'd never know the "fullness of the Spirit" until I spoke in tongues was a businessman whose life was full of sin. He insisted that I didn't know what the abundant life was all about. Little do we realize that the world looks at Christians and says, "If that's what it's all about, I don't want it!" How can we tell them that Jesus is the answer to life and yet not reflect it in our own lives.

This really baffled me, even after God had given me the beautiful gift of the Holy Spirit and a special language to communicate with Him. I began to search the scriptures more and more. Then the answer came so quickly I was amazed that I hadn't seen it before!

I had questioned many people in my search for the truth concerning this matter. "Can you be a carnal Christian and still speak in tongues?" Read I Corinthians where immorality and depravity ran rampant. Incest was there. Warring among the saints was there. Arguments and dissension were in the church. They were even quarreling about who belonged to whom. As Paul said in the first Chapter, 12th verse: "Now this I say, that every one of you saith, I am of Paul; and I of Apollos; and I of Cephas; and I of Christ. Is Christ divided? Was Paul crucified for you? Or were ye baptized in the name of Paul?" Here these Christians were arguing and squabbling like a bunch of little children. I especially love the Living New Testament's I Cor. 3:3: "For you are still only baby Christians, controlled by your own desires, not God's. When you are jealous of one another and divide up into quarreling groups, doesn't that prove you are still babies, wanting your own way? In fact, you are acting like people who don't belong to the Lord at all."

And don't we act the same way today? Paul goes on to say, "There you are, quarreling about whether I am greater than Apollos, and *dividing the church*. Doesn't this show how little you have grown in the Lord?"

Quarreling and dividing the church certainly

indicates a lack of godliness, doesn't it? Read what I Cor. 4:20 says about this: "The kingdom of God is not just talking; IT IS LIVING GOD'S POWER."

It's obvious that some people at Corinth spoke in tongues. Yet it is also obvious that they were not all living by God's power. Some were still living in the "flesh" and not being controlled by God. The ability to speak in tongues was apparently not withdrawn, in spite of their obvious sin and flaunting of God's laws, so scripturally it is completely possible to speak in tongues and still not be controlled by the Spirit all the time. This I believe is where some of the greatest problems begin. Many of the people who speak in tongues turn others off because of their insistence that this is their spiritual badge of holiness.

At this particular point in writing this book, I was stopped by a telephone call from a young married couple who were both ready to "throw their Christianity down the drain" because they felt the confusion in their lives caused by this issue was bringing them nothing but torment. My answer? I told them to seek God, the giver, and not the gifts, and this would bring the fruit of the Spirit which was what they were lacking in their lives.

A light finally began to break through as I shared the difference between the "gift" of tongues and the prayer tongue which accompanies the filling with the Holy Spirit. ALL began to speak in tongues when the "Holy Spirit fell on them," but not all have the "gift" of tongues, or the ability to receive a message from God in a public meeting and speak it to the rest of the church for interpretation.

They had never realized this before!

Other things became clear at this moment! Some of the Corinthians had been baptized with the Holy Spirit, and continued speaking in tongues even when their lives were carnal, carnal, CARNAL! God doesn't withdraw what He gives. So it is today! At that moment when we in total surrender give all of ourselves to God and ask for the gift of the Holy Spirit, He gives it to us with the scriptural evidence of speaking in tongues. It confirms this act. In water baptism we are submerged in the water and then brought out again, but the fact remains even when our clothes are dry, we have been baptized. It does not mean that we are continually in the water! The same thing is true of the Holy Spirit baptism. At the moment we ask for the baptism and are willing to receive it, the manifestation is there. Unless we stay dead to self, the outward manifestation of that first time baptism will still be there even though the inward manifestation can "dry up" just as your clothes got dry after your water baptism. We must continue daily, moment by moment, walking with God.

Read any translation that you like concerning the spiritual gifts. They all say the same thing. Paul wanted to make sure there was no ignorance, misunderstanding or misinformation concerning them. He starts out the 12th Chapter of I Corinthians specifically mentioning this: "And now, brothers, I want to write about the special abilities the Holy Spirit gives to each of you, for I don't want any misunderstanding about them."

Black and white—no gray—all black and white. He says he doesn't want ANY misunderstanding concerning them. And yet what other subject is more misunderstood than tongues? Each side is literally ripping the body of Christ apart by saying, "You don't have it—you don't speak in tongues," or "There is no such genuine gift."

No one can ever be baptized with the Holy Spirit before he is saved. The most supernatural gift of all is the gift of spiritual rebirth. Has God removed this from today's world? No, praise God! He certainly has not! It is the foundation for everything God has for His children thereafter. And nowhere in the Bible does it say that this ability to pray in the Spirit has been withdrawn from Christians today. There is no scripture that takes away this supernatural gift of God! And neither has He removed the power He promised, which He gave at Pentecost.

But neither does one then have to attain any spiritual level before they can receive the Holy Spirit. No one can ever become good enough to deserve either the gift of eternal life or the gift of the Holy Spirit. He gives the believer the extra spiritual power to become more like Christ.

CHAPTER 9

GET THOSE HANG-UPS OUT IN THE OPEN

"As the deer pants for water, so I long for you, O God. I thirst for God, the living God" (Psalms 42:l).

Let's look at hang-ups, shall we? We had about every hang-up in the book (and lots of them not in any book) concerning this particular manifestation of the baptism of the Holy Spirit. If you have few or many, little or big, scriptural (according to your teaching) or non-scriptural, praise God, and come along with us. We want to share with you how we finally got rid of the hang-ups we had concerning this beautiful gift of God. That verse of Psalms quoted above was the secret to God opening our eyes and revealing the simple and beautiful truth of His love. We continued to thirst for God, the living God, as a deer pants for water, and in thirsting for more and more of God, we came across the beautiful answer—the living water. You may discover, as we did, that God has recently "put a lot of new verses" in the Bible, or was it just because we didn't WANT to see them until recently!

It is amazing how we can zealously serve God,

love Him, desire to do whatever He wants us to, and yet be hung up on some particular doctrine or part of the scripture. We really have laughed at ourselves as we look back on this blind spot in our life, a total blindness to a real beautiful truth of God. We remember all the times we so energetically defended "our position" concerning tongues. Right now we're wondering whose position we were really defending. How could we have attempted to defend something we didn't know anything about? Have you ever been trapped the same way we were? Have you ever eaten your own words on something? Praise God, because when any of us realize that we do have "hang-ups," then we're on the road out of the "maze" and are now moving into the Promised Land.

One morning we came across a scripture and if you haven't opened the eyes of your own spirit to be receptive to what God has for you, listen: "Then Jesus told him 'I have come into the world to give sight to those who are spiritually blind and to SHOW THOSE WHO THINK THEY SEE THAT THEY ARE BLIND!'" (John 9:39). We really wondered if we were still spiritually blind in certain areas, and you know what? We discovered we were!

Isn't it exciting when you're submerged in Jesus you can honestly laugh at yourself and some of the things you formerly did? Isn't it amazing how easy it is to say, "I was wrong!" Did you ever try to admit that before you became a Christian? Honestly, did you ever grit your teeth and say, "I'll die before I'll ever admit I was wrong."

Would you like an honest admission from both of us right now? We were BOTH wrong in our understanding of this dimension and were wrong for a long time. We feared the unknown. Before we accepted Jesus as our Saviour and Lord, we were afraid of Christianity because it was an "unknown" thing to us. We were "afraid" of what we might have to give up if we became Christians. Finally we discovered the Truth, and again the truth set us free!

We were afraid of tongues because we didn't know anything about them. Praying in tongues was an "unknown" to us, so we were afraid of what it would do to us. As a matter of fact, we didn't even know that tongues had anything to do with prayer! After years of ignorance we discovered the truth. No longer was there fear! Fear in our hearts indicates we're not trusting God, doesn't it?

Are you hung up on words like we were? Do you immediately bristle at the thought that someone might be indicating that you have previously NOT been filled with the Holy Spirit? Oh, what a glorious time your pride can have with this! "I've been serving God all these years, I KNOW I've been filled with His Spirit!" "Don't tell me I haven't been controlled by the Holy Spirit!" "Look at my life, certainly MY WORKS should be proof I have been filled with the Holy Spirit."

Frances:

At this point I have to bring up something that really "bugged" me for a long time. How could I explain about my previous walk with God? I had prayed asking God to fill me with His Holy Spirit. Would God have denied my request? I don't believe so; however, was I refusing to accept His answer because I was unwilling to surrender the most unruly member of my body, my tongue?

Harald Bredesen told us an interesting story which we'd like to share with you. It very simply and beautifully expresses a truth about the situation. At the start of the Catholic Pentecostal movement, three of the brothers from Duquesne University who had been baptized with the Holy Spirit held a retreat with 31 students, to study the baptism with the Holy Spirit. They were apparently not making too much progress and decided to take time out for lunch. The retreat was held in a camp which was not used too often. As they started to prepare lunch, they turned on the water faucet, but couldn't get any water.

They informed the owners of the camp, who then told them the well was dry. The retreat was making too little progress anyway, so they decided after this problem to call it off. Finally one of them said, "If Jesus was here, what would He do?" They all knew, so they began to pray. First they praised God, then they petitioned Him and asked Him to miraculously fill the well, and finally thanked Him (in faith) for having filled the well. Then one of the brothers went to the faucet and turned on the spigot. The water gushed out!

Do you see it?

What good did it do them to have the well filled, if they didn't turn on the spigot?

Is this the same thing that happened to me? I asked God to fill me and I believed then that He was ready to, but what good did it do me until I was willing to turn on the spigot and let the living water flow from my innermost being. (See John 7:38)

Many people are just sitting there today with a cork holding back the power from on high. The tongue (so to speak) is like a cork which keeps the Holy Spirit held back, and keeps the living water from flowing.

Listen to what God says about being thirsty. "And the joy of the Lord shall fill you full; you shall glory in the God of Israel. When the poor and needy seek water and there is none and their tongues are parched from thirst, then I will answer when they cry to me. I, Israel's God, will not ever forsake them. I will open up rivers for them on high plateaus! I will give them fountains of water in the valleys! In the deserts will be pools of water, and rivers fed by springs shall flow across the dry parched ground. I will plant trees—cedars, myrtle, olive trees, the cypress, fir and pine—on barren land. Everyone will see this miracle and understand that it is God who did it, Israel's Holy One" (Isaiah 41:16-20).

God is calling us out of the desert to the fountains that never shall run dry!

There's an endless number of quotes which both of us have either said or thought, but Praise God that Heaven could be carpeted wall to wall with rugs the Lord has jerked out from under us.

Too often we are "carpet-beggars"—we want the old rugs back to stand on again instead of trusting Him all the way. We remember how many times we have said, "We don't need tongues." How do we know what's best for us? Only God knows that, and how we love Him for not listening to some of the foolish talk we gave Him.

Here's a real gem! "Those 'tongues' people always act so superior like they're better than we are!" We just have to quote something that Ralph Marinacci, a beautiful friend of ours, said at our house one night: "This doesn't make me any better than YOU are, but it makes me better than I was." Isn't that a beautiful thought? We really had our "hear muffs" on the night he said that. Did you ever wear "hear-not muffs?" We both did for a long time where the baptism was concerned. The thing to do is to listen to the doctor (great Physician), and not the doctrine, and honestly see what God has to say about any matter.

We have listened to some really interesting arguments at various phases of our Christian lives. Arguing is one thing we are careful not to do, because we remember Paul's words to Timothy which are personalized in our Bibles to us, and so the 6th Chapter, vs 20-21 reads: "Oh, Frances and Charles, don't fail to do these things that God has entrusted to you. Keep out of foolish arguments with those who boast of their 'knowledge' and thus prove their lack of it. Some of these people have missed the most important thing in life—they don't know God." Arguing accomplishes nothing for either side, but gets everybody upset and then Satan really has a field day. If someone doesn't agree with us, we just say,

"Praise God!"

Do you have a hang-up about praying in the Spirit being emotional? We did, and if you do, we'd like you to think about a few little statements. You're right, there is emotion, but wait a minute as we share about how emotion plays a great part in all of our lives.

Do you talk to those you love without any emotion at all? Do you say, "I love you" to your husband, wife, children or any other person in a dull monotone without any emotion? Even when we speak of food, we often say, "I love hot fudge sundaes," or, "I'd love to have a real cold glass of lemonade." Do you say that in an absolutely emotionless voice? Isn't there enthusiasm (or emotionalism) in your voice when you say "I LOVE hot fudge sundaes?"

Can you imagine what life would be like if we all went around without any emotion? Can you imagine how dull and uninteresting the English language would be if we never expressed some emotion? What if there were no exclamation marks! What do you call the reaction of a crowd during a football game? Is that emotion?. . .and how about a wedding? Recently we went to one of the most beautiful weddings we have ever attended. The minister asked the usual question, "Who gives this woman away?" and her daddy replied, "I do." As he relinquished his daughter to her soon-to-be husband, he lifted the edge of her veil, and planted on her cheek the most beautiful father-daughter kiss you could imagine. You'd better believe every person in that

church was emotional! Was that bad? No it wasn't!
It was beautiful!

The Bible says: "And thou shalt love the Lord
thy God with all thine heart, and with all thy soul,
and with all thy might." How can love like that be
unemotional? It just can't be! So isn't it all right to
admit that praying in the Spirit is emotional too? It's
tied up with the love of God! And our love of God is
worthy of emotion. You can't LOVE God without
having some emotion!

Did anyone ever tell you that you can pray silently in tongues? When a situation arises where you
need fervent prayer in a hurry for a crisis you don't
fully understand, you can pray in the Spirit without
uttering a sound. And you can pray without even
having to think what you're praying, because the
Holy Spirit who knows all things prays for you. One
of the awakenings we had was the knowledge that
we could stop or start at will.

Did you ever have the hang-up we did about the
fear of just bursting out with tongues when it might
embarrass you to death?

So often I've heard the remark, "If tongues are
from God, how can you stop and start at will?
Wouldn't you just break out in it at any time without
realizing it? If it's God speaking, how can you shut it
off?" That's an interesting question. If I praise God
in English I can stop and start at will. Why shouldn't
it be the same with tongues? In the same way as our
tongue in English is under our control, so is the utterance of our own special "love" language controlled by us. We can start and stop as we desire. We

always control our own vocal chords, but the language is controlled by the Holy Spirit.

The beautiful thing about God and His love is that He never removes from us the privilege of exercising our own will. By our own free choice we can WILL to follow Him, or we can WILL to follow the devil. He never forces Himself upon us, but gives us our own free choice. And when He blesses us with the ability to praise Him in an unknown tongue, He still does not violate our will. Any individual who praises God in tongues can WILL to start and can WILL to stop. Isn't it ridiculous to think that the Holy Spirit is anything but a gentleman who waits until we WILL to speak in tongues? Then when we WILL to stop, He allows us to do just that. We've heard pastors say, "If God wants me to speak in tongues, then I'm sure He will give it to me, and all of a sudden I'll start talking in tongues." Again, the Holy Spirit is such a perfect gentleman, He would never force Himself upon us against our own will.

Well, now let's see, what's another classic hang-up? How about those who say that tongues are divisive? How many times have we heard this! You're right—tongues can really divide a church—if *BOTH* sides are wrong. One side says it's not of God, and the other side might say you just haven't "got it" unless you speak in tongues.

We look back at what irritated us about "tongues" people, and find the divisiveness was because "we" didn't believe what "they" believed! We had not received the baptism with the Holy Spirit, so how could we know? We wanted NO part of them.

It was we who argued against them in our ignorance—not them against us!

Misuse of the gift or a superior attitude can be divisive, but the Holy Spirit isn't divisive. It's only attitudes that are divisive—not God's gifts.

How many congregations have been split apart by doctrines other than tongues? How many churches have been split apart because half the congregation approved of the pastor, and the other half did not? How many churches have been split because of disagreement over a building fund drive? How many leaders of churches have left because of disapproval of the youth program? Even today, how many churches are being split apart because of the refusal of the "old timers" to accept the sincerity of the young people in the great JESUS movement that is sweeping across our country? How often do people thwart the Spirit of God moving in a church because of a dogmatic attitude? How many people refuse to change "because we've always done it this way" and thus bring division.

"Don't rock our 50 year old boat."

And so you're right, tongues can be divisive, if not properly taught and understood by all concerned, and if not properly used.

But then, so can a lot of other things. Have you ever thought of that?

Most all of us who are "professing" Christians are hung up on one thing or another. Many of the churches we've attended are really hung up on their particular denomination instead of on Jesus. They talk about their particular church and not the fact that JESUS is the answer to life!

And then you have the "busy" Christian—the one who gets so involved in doing all the "little" things in a church that he hasn't any time left for God. He has a real hang-up because he's forgotten the Giver and seeks after the personal glory that comes from having all the titles and responsibilities in a church.

One of the real "hang-ups" of the charismatic movement is because it's so enjoyable, so exciting, so moving, so personal, so holy and uplifting, so enveloping, loving and beautiful that we just want to enjoy it all the time, sometimes to the exclusion of our other Christian responsibilities. We get so caught up in what it does for our own personal life, that we forget the Great Commission of the Bible is to share the Good News of Jesus, not just the gifts of the Holy Spirit.

Speaking in tongues is not the road to Heaven for we are told that Jesus is the way—the ONLY way! It is, however, spiritually valuable here on earth because it helps build our faith. We could not speak in a beautiful love language without being constantly increased in faith, knowing that such a supernatural sign is a gift from God.

"There's so much misunderstanding about praying in the Spirit, or speaking in tongues." This is a real hang-up and keeps many people from going on, but instead of stopping, we should investigate for ourselves and see what *God* has to say.

Frances

I was sitting at my desk opening the morning mail when the telephone rang and I answered in my usual manner, "Good morning, God is Fabulous!" During the next ten minutes I discovered how some people feel about the other side of the coin. I could scarcely believe my ears as a pastor who had known me for years identified himself and then said, "I understand that George Otis said when he spoke in Alaska that you now speak in tongues." George Otis had shared the fact that the Lord had blessed us with the wonderful gift of the Holy Spirit in the same way we've shared when someone has accepted Christ.

The friendliness vanished from my caller's voice. He demanded: "Is the information correct? Frances, do you speak in tongues?" It was suddenly as cold as if someone had put icicles on the telephone wire. I prayed for great love and wisdom. I said, "God in His wonderful and exciting plan for my life, has given me another of His perfect gifts, and since ALL of the gifts of God are good, I have accepted the baptism with the Holy Spirit in the same love as I have accepted the gift of eternal life."

Very coldly he said, "Then we won't be able to have you at our church next week, because the meeting just wouldn't have the right spirit!"

I explained to him that I respect the rights of all churches. I felt as if I was on a witness stand being tried for murder, and he was the accuser. He condemned me without examination. I told him that at every meeting, club, or church where I had spoken since receiving the baptism there were people who had heard me speak before. Everywhere, WITHOUT EXCEPTION, I've heard the same comment: "Frances there's more POWER in your talks than I've ever heard before. It seems like there's a whole new dimension." Up until this point God had never led us to take a public stand, although everyone who asked us outright received an honest answer.

My heart broke, because all I could think of was what sorrow misunderstanding can cause us—misunderstanding because we haven't honestly opened ourselves to God to let Him reveal the truth concerning certain passages in the Bible. Following the rut of tradition can be deadly at times! The very fact that God had met me in this way did not in any way stop me from being a child of God! As a matter of fact, the new dimension brought me even closer and closer to God.

Why wasn't there the same joy in that pastor at my accepting the baptism with the Holy Spirit as there was when I was saved? Is the gift to be despised?

We misunderstand because we don't really get into God's Word and read and accept what He has to say. I know in my own life when I was really turned off on tongues in the beginning, I ignored reading the parts of the Bible that were about it. I had read them once and read into them exactly the doctrine of the church I attended, and nothing else. I never asked God to show me. Only after I was willing to let God reveal what He had for my life, did the misunderstanding about tongues begin to disappear.

We'd like to earnestly suggest if you have been one of those (like us) who never really understood the difference between the gift of the Holy Spirit and the "gift" of tongues, that you clear your mind of everything you've heard concerning this gift. Ask God to teach you from His Word about it. Ask Him if it is no longer needed in this day and age! (When has it ever been needed more?) Was it withdrawn when the last apostle died?—Do you want to tell Him that you don't need it?—That you don't want it?—Is there no purpose in it? If you honestly want more of God, we'd suggest that you start reaching out to Jesus, asking Him to meet you in truth on this subject. Then get into your Bible and see what happens.

It may be that because you have been willing to accept the beliefs of someone else instead of going directly to God's Word, you are denying yourself this heavenly gift. What do you as an individual honestly KNOW about this gift? Be honest—not what have you *heard* about this subject, but what do you honestly KNOW? For my first six years as a Christian, I only knew the opinions of other people. Now I know what God says about this, and it's beautiful! And how I praise Him because he opened up my mind and cleared out the cobwebs of misunderstanding.

We firmly believe anyone who sincerely is seeing all that God has for them will eventually discover the reality and validity of praising God in the Spirit!

We'd like to ask you once again—have you honestly taken all of your hang-ups out of the closet?

(We even threw away the hangers in our house). Take a real good look at any reason you have and see if you still feel the same way. If so, pray right now that God will remove any hang-up that keeps you from the exciting, abundant Christian life. And above all else, remember to be honest with yourself, because you can't be honest with God until you are honest with yourself.

Even if you feel you have no need, would you be willing to let God prove Himself to you in a new way? Probably one of the biggest hang-ups today is when we feel we have no further needs. As you know from reading this book, this is the way we felt, and yet there was a need there that we didn't realize. How we praise God He got rid of that hang-up, too.

Think about this! (from Frances):

I was lying in bed one morning, completely awake. I had been up and prepared Charles' breakfast, but had gone back to bed to read the Bible and meditate upon the exact meaning of the expression "baptism in the Holy Spirit." Suddenly it became vividly clear. I was awake—my mind thinking in all directions—talking to God—praying—but my eyes were closed, so there was a part of the picture I did not see even though I was awake. Was I really awake? I did not have all the "signs" of being awake, because anyone coming into the room would have thought I was asleep, but the sign would have been opening my eyes, or making a sound. So are tongues an audible sign of the activities of the Spirit.

And this (from Charles):

Is the sign, speaking in tongues, an essential ingredient of baptism with the Holy Spirit? Is it important to salvation to *tell* others the good news—to show the unsaved the way to eternal life through Jesus? Romans 10:8—"For salvation that comes from trusting Christ—which is what we preach—is already within easy reach of each of us; in fact, it is as near as our own hearts and mouths. FOR IF YOU TELL OTHERS WITH YOUR OWN MOUTH that Jesus Christ is Lord, and believe in your own heart that God has raised him from the dead, you will be saved. For it is by believing in his heart that a man becomes right with God; and with his MOUTH he tells others of his faith, CONFIRMING HIS SALVATION. For the Scriptures tell us that no one who believes in Christ will ever be disappointed."

Now look at these verses: Acts 10:45-47: "The Jews who came with Peter were amazed that the gift of the Holy Spirit would be given to Gentiles, too! But there could be no doubt about it, for they heard them SPEAKING IN TONGUES and praising God." Acts 15:8. . ."God, who knows men's hearts, CONFIRMED the fact that He accepts Gentiles by giving them the Holy Spirit, just as he gave Him to us." Notice how both salvation and baptism are confirmed by our mouth, or our tongue, which is our speech mechanism.

So many people have the hang-up of, "Well, do you HAVE to speak in tongues?" I love the answer given by Warren Black, Comptroller for the Nazarene Church, as stated in the June, 1972 issue of Voice, "You *can't* speak in tongues until you are baptized with the Holy Spirit, then it's a privilege."

How true, how true!

If you've gotten rid of your hang-ups, then you're ready for the next part of this book. Hallelujah!

CHAPTER 10

THE "GIFT" OF TONGUES

The nine gifts, as mentioned previously, might also be considered as "jobs" or spiritual capabilities which God has given to certain people. Many people feel we have the choice of selecting whether we want the gifts or the fruit, because they don't understand the difference. Gifts are given by God for His glory and as an extension of the ministry of Jesus. The fruit of the Spirit is the result of being possessed completely by the Holy Spirit. The fruit is promised when we are controlled by the Holy Spirit. The only gift we're going to touch on in this chapter is the gift of tongues which has been misunderstood by so many. Because I was among the many who misunderstood this gift, I asked God to reveal something real special to me in the scriptures that would convince both sides, and as I read I Cor. 12th chapter, starting with the 13th verse, it really spoke to me.

I quote from the Living Bible because it is easy for everyone to understand, but you may refer to any translation of the Bible you enjoy and read, and it will say basically the same thing. I am quoting it, even though it is long, because I think it might clarify a point for anyone who reads this book.

"Each of us is a part of the one body of Christ. Some of us are Jews, some are Gentiles, some are slaves and some are free. But the Holy Spirit has fitted us all together into one body. We have been baptized into Christ's body by the one Spirit, and have all been given that same Holy Spirit.

"Yes, the body has many parts, not just one part. If the foot says, 'I am not a part of the body because I am not a hand,' that does not make it any less a part of the body. And what would you think if you heard an ear say, 'I am not part of the body because I am only an ear, and not an eye'? Would that make it any less a part of the body? Suppose the whole body were an eye—then how would you hear? Or if your whole body were just one big ear, how could you smell anything? But that isn't the way God has made us. He has made many parts for our bodies and has put each part just where he wants it. What a strange thing a body would be if it had only one part! So he has made many parts, but still there is only one body. The eye can never say to the hand, 'I don't need you.' The head can't say to the feet, 'I don't need you.' And some of the parts that seem weakest and least important are really the most necessary. Yes, we are especially glad to have some parts that seem rather odd! And we carefully protect from the eyes of other those parts that should not be seen, while of course the parts that may be seen do not require this special care. So God has put the body together in such a way that extra honor and care are given to those parts that might otherwise seem less important. This makes for happiness among the parts, so that the parts have the same care for each other that they do for themselves. If one part suffers, all parts suffer with it, and if one part is honored, all the parts are glad.

"Now here is what I am trying to say: All of you together are the one body of Christ and each one of you is a separate and necessary part of it. Here is a list of some of the parts he has placed in his church, which is his body:

Apostles,

Prophets—those who preach God's Word,

Teachers,

Those who do miracles,

Those who have the gift of healing,

Those who can help others,

Those who can get others to work together,

Those who speak in languages they have never learned. Is everyone an apostle? Of course not. Is everyone a preacher? No. Are all teachers? Does everyone have the power to do miracles? Can everyone heal the sick? Of course not. Does God give all of us the ability to speak in languages we've never learned? Can just anyone understand and translate what those are saying who have that gift of foreign speech? No, but try your best to have the more important of these gifts."

What God showed me in this particular passage of scripture was confirmation of the fact "we have been baptized into Christ's body by the one Spirit, and have all been given that same Holy Spirit." There is only one Spirit which we have all been given. All the parts of the body belong to the body, and none of them has the right to separate themselves from the rest of the body. Think of your own physical body—would you throw your ear away and say, "I don't want you because I don't like your looks?" No, because whether you like it or not, it is a part of your physical body. Would you throw one of your legs away because you don't like it? Would you say, "You don't belong to this body—I don't want you around?" No, because your body would be seriously handicapped without that leg.

So it is with the Body of Christ. Read what it says concerning the list of some of the parts He has placed in His church, which is His body: Can we say to each other, "I don't want anyone who is an apostle around me, because that gift isn't of God!" No, because the apostle is a part of the Body of Christ. Can we say the same thing about prophets—those who preach God's Word? No, because they are a part of Christ's body, just as the apostles are. Go right down the list and see if there is any scriptural authority anyone has for throwing out of the body of Christ "THOSE WHO SPEAK IN LANGUAGES THEY HAVE NEVER LEARNED." Paul says, "The eye can never say to the hand, 'I don't need you.' The Head can't say to the feet, 'I don't need you.'" Neither can the apostle say to the tongues speaker, "I don't need you."

A part of the scripture that especially spoke to my heart was the part that starts with verse 22. "And some of the parts that seem weakest and least important are really the most necessary. Yes we are especially glad to have some parts that seem rather odd. And we carefully protect from the eyes of others those parts that should not be seen, while of course the parts that may be seen do not require this special care."

Often I have heard the gift of tongues referred to as the least desirable of the gifts because it is listed last. If that has been your thinking, see what it says about the weakest and least important being really the most necessary. Some people think this gift is "odd." Even in our own physical bodies, we protect the parts that should not be seen by others, and Paul says to do the same thing in our spiritual lives. In the 14th Chapter you will see what he has to say about speaking in tongues privately which is really "carefully protecting from the eyes of others those parts that should not be seen." Tongues are given mainly to build up the faith of the individual and should be treasured as a personal prize and protected from those who don't understand or don't care to understand.

Isn't it beautiful how the famous LOVE chapter of the Bible (I Cor., 13th chapter) rests snugly between the two chapters which deal with this most controversial subject? To each side God is saying, "Love is better than any of the gifts. Even if you have all the gifts, they are nothing without love." Isn't he saying to the person who speaks in an unknown language without love it is nothing but noise? And what good is noise?

If we say to our brother or sister in Christ, "You are inferior because you do not speak in tongues" we would be just making noise because it wouldn't be said in love. Neither can the other side say, "You are inferior or dangerous because you speak in tongues." If there is REAL God-love on both sides, each will honor the other side.

Let's see what Paul goes on to say about this matter of speaking in tongues. He says in the 14th chapter, verse 5, "I wish you all had the gift of 'speaking in tongues'".... There's more to the verse, but now I just want to remind you that Paul said he wished every single one of us had the gift of tongues. Why? Because look what he says in verse 18 about thanking God that "I 'speak in tongues' privately more than any of the rest of you." He knew how much it built up his own faith, and he wished every single person would take advantage of this provision of the Lord to build up his own faith.

The classic scripture excuse (and I used it many times myself) is "I would much rather speak five words that people can understand and be helped by, than ten thousand words while 'speaking in tongues' in an unknown language." That's so right for *public use,* but where did he say *not* to speak the ten thousand words in an unknown tongue? Nowhere. As a matter of fact the very last verse in the 14th chapter of I Corinthians takes care of this very well because it says: "never say it is wrong to 'speak in tongues;' (God! when did you put that in the Bible?) however, be sure that everything is done properly in a good and orderly way."

How much plainer can the Bible get? I have since wondered if I had ever read that chapter all the way through. If so, how could I have even thought it was wrong to speak in tongues? How blind I was!

There are parts of our own bodies that are used more than others. As I sit at my typewriter writing books, my fingers are used far more than my legs, but I certainly appreciate my legs when I get up from the typewriter. Toes are also rather funny looking if you look at them real closely, but I wonder how easy it would be to stand if we didn't have toes. They're necessary, too. Feet aren't especially beautiful, either, but they are certainly vital to my being able to get around. So it is with the different parts of the body of Christ. Some are used more than others and all are used in different ways. Praise God! Wouldn't it be terrible if we were all used in exactly the same way?

I like the way Paul gives the answer to this question in I Corinthians 14:15: "Well, then what shall I do? I WILL DO BOTH. I will pray in unknown tongues and also in ordinary language that everyone understands. I will sing in unknown tongues and also in ordinary language, so that I can understand the praise I am giving." That is just what we do! When I am alone in the house during the daytime, I praise God in English and I praise Him in "His" language. I sing in English, and I sing in the Spirit, and have a marvelous time both ways. Each way lifts my spirit in a different manner. Neither is better. Both are best!

Jesus was the perfect lamb, without spot or blemish. How can He be perfect in us if we amputate one part of His body?

CHAPTER 11

WHY THE BAPTISM
WITH THE HOLY SPIRIT—
IS IT REALLY NECESSARY?

These two questions have been asked us probably more than any other questions. We'll try to answer them in this chapter. Few of us actually understand what the work of the Holy Spirit is.

When Jesus died, He knew very well the weaknesses of each of the disciples. He knew that even though they had walked with Him, lived with Him, and eaten with Him, they still had no real power in their lives. "During the 40 days after His crucifixion He had appeared to the apostles from time to time in human form and proved to them in many ways that it was actually He Himself they were seeing. On such occasions He talked to them about the Kingdom of God. In one of these meetings He told them not to leave Jerusalem until the Holy Spirit came upon them in fulfillment of the Father's promise, a matter He had previously discussed with them. 'John baptized you with water,' He reminded them, 'but you shall be baptized with the Holy Spirit in just a few days'" (Acts 1:3-5). Then there was His great promise in Acts 1:8: "But when the Holy Spirit has come upon you, you will receive power to preach with great effect to the people in Jerusalem, through Judea, in Samaria, and to the ends of the earth, about my death and resurrection." He didn't say that SOME would receive power. He said that YOU, meaning ALL of you, would receive power when the Holy Spirit has come upon you.

And power does come when we are willing and prepared to receive it—power to live the Christian life, power to be the man or woman God wants us to be—power to be used by God. "Power to be" is a-vailable when we are obedient to God. Jesus told the disciples to go into the upper room and tarry until they were filled with the Holy Spirit, and not to go right out to testify. They were obedient to Him. They *wanted* to do exactly what Jesus instructed them to do. They were open to receiving the power Jesus had promised. EVERYONE present was filled with the Holy Spirit and began immediately speaking in lan-guages they didn't know, for the Holy Spirit gave them this ability.

Jesus had given them the Great Commission to share the Good News, and now He enabled them to do so by delivering the power He had promised, and EVERYONE was filled!

Galatians 5:16-25 really expresses a lot about the ministry of the Holy Spirit. "I advise you to obey only the Holy Spirit's instructions. He will tell you where to go and what to do, and then you won't al-ways be doing the wrong things your evil nature wants you to. For we naturally love to do evil things that are just the opposite from the things that the Holy Spirit tells us to do; and the good things we want to do when the Spirit has His way with us are just the opposite of our natural desires. These two forces within us are constantly fighting each other to win control over us, and our wishes are never free from their pressures. When you are guided by the Holy Spirit you need no longer force yourself to obey Jewish laws. But when you follow your own wrong inclinations your lives will produce these evil results: impure thoughts, eagerness for lustful pleasure, idolatry, spiritism (that is, encouraging the activity of demons), hatred and fighting, jealousy and anger, constant effort to get the best for yourself, complaints and criticisms, the feeling that everyone else is wrong except those in your own little group—and there will be wrong doctrine, envy, murder, drunkenness, wild parties, and all that sort of thing. Let me tell you again as I have before, that anyone living that sort of life will not inherit the kingdom of God.

"But when the Holy Spirit controls our lives he will produce this kind of fruit in us: love, joy, peace, patience, kindness, goodness, faithfulness, gentleness, and self-control; and here there is no conflict with Jewish laws. Those who belong to Christ have nailed their natural evil desires to His cross and crucified them there.

"IF WE ARE NOW LIVING BY THE HOLY SPIRIT'S POWER, LET US FOLLOW THE HOLY SPIRIT'S LEADING IN EVERY PART OF OUR

LIVES. THEN WE WON'T NEED TO LOOK FOR
HONORS AND POPULARITY, WHICH LEAD TO
JEALOUSY AND HARD FEELINGS."
Let's compare the two kinds of lives.

SPIRIT-CONTROLLED PRODUCES:
Love
Joy
Peace
Patience
Kindness
Goodness
Faithfulness
Gentleness
Self-Control

NON-SPIRIT-CONTROLLED (OR CARNAL)
IS VULNERABLE TO:
Impure thoughts
Eagerness for lustful pleasure
     (things of the world)
Idolatry
Spiritism
Hatred and fighting
Jealousy and anger
Constant effort to get the best
     for yourself
Complaints and criticisms
The feeling that everyone else is
     wrong except those in your
     own little group
Wrong doctrine
Envy

Murder

Drunkenness

Wild parties

When you look at the list on the non-Spirit-controlled life, you might have a tendency to say, "Well, that's not me, I don't drink, and I don't murder." A friend of ours recently said, "All of a sudden I realized that they were all separated by only a *comma.*"

Impure thoughts are not all concerning sex, as a lot of people seem to think, but in this category comes that common Christian sin of worry. The Bible says, "why be like the heathen?" And yet Christians do worry. Any worrying thought is an impure thought and shows a lack of trust in God. Just check down the list and grade yourself!

The baptism with the Holy Spirit and the ability to speak in tongues is not a cure-all, nor a pass to get off of the roller coaster ride on which many Christians find themselves: high spiritually one moment, and then down in the valley the next! But it is power for your Christian growth. It is for many "the fountainhead of meaning and vitality, a direct contact with God." It is for many the teeth which enables them to eat spiritual meat instead of staying on milk. It is the catalyst into the abundant exciting Christian life, if you want it to be.

The Holy Spirit is the one who will lead you and guide you to all truth and give you the power you need.

*WHY THE BAPTISM?*Because God understood the frailties of human nature. He knew that man in his finite human strength could never live the Christian life. This is why God gave Jesus the authority to send back the Holy Spirit. This is why Jesus told the disciples to wait until He sent back the Holy Spirit. This was the changing point in their lives. Never again were they defeated! And neither do you need to ever be defeated again!

WHY THE BAPTISM? In our own personal lives it has done many things. For the first time we are now better able to praise God in the manner He deserves. The Holy Spirit came to glorify Christ, and if we are filled with the Holy Spirit we will glorify Christ, we will worship Him and lift Him up. Our daughter Joan said, "It enables you to talk to God on His level instead of your own level."

WHY THE BAPTISM? Because of what it does for your prayer life. There is a prayer dynamic which we never dreamed was possible. We had wondered how our prayer life could possibly be more fervent when we didn't understand what we were saying. We discovered it was impossible—to man—but NOT TO GOD. He, and He alone, gives you the freedom for more fervency (and we don't mean emotionalism).

One of the things both of us really appreciate about praying in the Spirit is when the Holy Spirit puts into our minds the names of people, places, circumstances, dates, etc., we know at that exact moment that person is being prayed for by the Spirit on our new "hot line" to heaven. Many times we do not know the need of the person who has been recalled to our mind, but the Holy Spirit does.

WHY THE BAPTISM? Has there ever been a time when you honestly didn't know HOW to pray? We have just gone through such a situation. Praying in tongues in times of urgent need reduces you to a place of complete reliance and trust. The Spirit can pray without interference from our cluttered mind. Oh, how many prayers we have seen answered because of this in recent months.

WHY THE BAPTISM? It has given us a better understanding of the spiritual meaning of scriptures, a greater desire to see people get beyond the defeated life and into the abundant life. It has increased our desire for Bible reading. It has provided great guidance and understanding of God's will for our lives.

WHY THE BAPTISM? Charles says: "It removed the veil, which dimmed my vision of Jesus." Frances: "It gave me a greater ability to love God more than I had ever had before. I had always accepted His love for me, but never had I been able to return it the way I wanted to. The baptism with the Holy Spirit released the love for God in my life."

WHY THE BAPTISM? Because it's scriptural!

CHAPTER 12

WHAT IS THE CHARISMATIC MOVEMENT?

"'In the last days,' God said, 'I will pour out my Holy Spirit upon all mankind, and your sons and daughters shall prophesy, and your young men shall see visions, and your old men dream dreams. Yes, the Holy Spirit shall come upon all my servants, men and women alike, and they shall prophesy'" (Acts 2:17).

The word "charisma" refers to the gifts of the Spirit, all of which are being revived with the great outpouring of the Holy Spirit in these times. For years the Pentecostal and the Main Line churches have been at odds with each other. God is pouring out His Holy Spirit on His people in all denominations today. The charismatic movement is helping to heal the breach between the Pentecostal and the Non-Pentecostal. There should never be harsh attitudes among Christians, regardless of the denomination. If we really believe that God's love flows through us, then we should act like it, and there should never be an attitude of anything except love.

God is uniting His people into a single unity of

believers today, not by a great merger of denominations, but by the uniting bond of the Holy Spirit
within the hearts of people inside the denomination.
The oneness of the Spirit dims our view of doctrinal
differences.

One of the most exciting things about the
charismatic movement which is causing the BIG
surge in this direction is the relaxed attitude of the
participants. Everyone seems to have expanded his
knowledge of a personal relationship with Jesus;
there is more joy, there is more worship of God,
there is more sharing of the Good News of Jesus. A
bigger harvest for salvation! No longer does there
seem to be a reluctance to talk about Jesus in every
walk of life. See those blossoming bumper stickers
and badges, too?

Many of the groups that we have met want to
share what Jesus has done in their lives; not telling
what Jesus did long ago, but all of the current little
miracles. They bubble with a love for Jesus! No
longer is Jesus some faraway removed being that
we'll get to be with when we die, but Jesus is ALIVE
today! Many still have never known the joy of being
the new baby in Christ who has been swept into the
Kingdom on the crest of this new wave of surfing in
the Spirit. And the only way you can stay on a wave
is to ride it right on the top!

There's excitement in the air, there's a genuineness to the talk, "He's Coming Again!" People are
saying it because they really mean it, not just because someone tells them to sing it in their church on
Sunday morning. People are excited talking about

the return of Jesus because they're READY for it.
They're expecting Him right now! We rode in a car
the other day with a bumper sticker which read
"Maranatha—What a way to go!" And somehow or
other there was a real joy just getting into that car!

Some of the most beautiful love we've ever seen
exhibited is the love in the charismatic movement.
They seem genuinely in love with their fellow man
and are ready to help the needy. Even when you
walk into a meeting, large or small, you are aware of
a tremendous love of God. It's beautiful! There's always the feeling of, "I'll share with you what I've
got," not, "Look what I've got that you haven't got!"
There's always a feeling of, "Come on in, the water's
fine, and there's room for all." There's always a feeling of, "I wonder what fabulous thing God is going
to do tonight?" It seems among the charismatic
people there is a real longing to be with other Christians, a real desire to get together and study the
Bible. There seems to be little reluctance to invite
non-charismatic friends to this type of meeting, because something beautiful always happens.

We have wanted to conduct a Bible study in our
home ever since we were married, and this year we
did. While it was a good growing period for all of us,
we noticed one very interesting thing. The moment
we concluded the Bible Study and then announced
that we would be sharing the baptism with the Holy
Spirit the next week, our house was filled to capacity! Previously we had averaged about 20 to 25 per
Bible Study. The very next meeting we had was
standing room only, as many people sat on the floor

or stood for almost four hours. Every time we are in Houston between trips long enough to let the word go out that we are having a meeting, our house is jammed to capacity! People are hungry for the baptism with fire! People are hungry for the power to make them what God wants them to be. People are hungry for a total commitment of their lives and this hunger seems to be predominantly grounded or rooted in the charismatic movement. One typical night we had about 70 in our home, which is certainly straining at the seams with that many people.

What do we do? We sing a little, pray a lot, share miracles between this week and last week, invite anyone who doesn't know Jesus to accept Him, share about the baptism with the Holy Spirit, and then we pray for specific needs. Not always in this order, but as the Holy Spirit directs.

People have been freed from the bondage of cigarettes, alcohol, adultery, the occult and many other things. It's amazing how these habits of long standing can be stopped in the twinkling of an eye by God's Spirit when people are praying. Recently a man was healed of asthma from which he had suffered most of his life. Just as he was leaving, he casually asked if we would pray for his healing. Immediately someone brought a chair, he sat down and all the men laid hands on him. Some prayed in English, and some prayed in the Spirit. When he got out of the chair, he was staggering under the power of God, and someone said it reminded him of the day of Pentecost when everyone thought those who had tarried in the Upper Room were drunk. They were—

not with wine, but with the Power of the Holy Spirit. This man felt the same way when God's healing power touched him. He says he has taken no medication since that time, and looks better than we've ever seen him. Cigarette smokers are set free by the simple ministry of a Christian praying "in the name of Jesus." People are hung up on reading their horoscope daily trying to find out what's best for them to do, instead of trusting God. This is a real abomination to the Lord and certainly He's pleased when people are made aware of the fact that this is a sin!

Scores are accepting Jesus in our home in surroundings where there is a genuine love of God. They are finding a relaxation in learning about the charisma (gifts of the Spirit). There is just a presentation of what happened to us (and the "us" can be any of the couples who come regularly) and then a relaxed feeling of if you want to accept, great, if not, that's up to you. There is no pressure, no hitting on the head (we used to think this is what "they" did to you), no arguing, just the beautiful love of God sweeping throughout the entire meeting. People are finding what everyone really wants—A LIVING JESUS!

Here's a little letter I felt impressed to share with you. The letter is dated June 9, 1972:

"Dear Frances,

"Ed and I received such a tremendous blessing when we heard you speak at Bethany Christian Church. I felt I just must write and *try* to tell you what you mean to us.

"Through you, our lives have been changed completely! For this I want to thank you from the bottom of my heart.

"The first time I read some of your books was in September, 1971. I reviewed GOD IS FABULOUS for our church round table. Since then I've reread and "re" reread them all so many times. There's hardly a day that goes by that I don't have a chance to tell someone about your fabulous books.

"From the very first I've never felt a more kindred feeling toward anyone. I kept feeling that in *some* way you were going to play a big part in my life. I didn't understand the feeling. . .we had never met and surely never would.

"When I heard you speak at the Keswick Luncheon the Lord formed the impression in my mind, 'you're going to meet this glorious lady some-day.'

"Months later I learned you were to speak to the Westchester High School Bible classes. I had a talk with the Lord. It went something like this: 'Lord, if this close feeling I've had and this desire to meet Frances Hunter is Your prompting then I'm going to pray a prayer of thanksgiving for allowing this to happen.' And just to hold the Lord to it, I wrote Him a thank you note in advance. This is the exact copy:

Thurs.2:00 April 6, 1972
Thank you Lord for allowing me to go to
Frances Hunter's home for prayer, for
talking with her, for becoming a friend of
hers. PTL soon, soon, Lord.

"I suppose the note went airmail because look

what happened! On April 12th I was at Westchester High School and heard you give your testimony to all three classes. When you finished, I astounded myself by asking you out to eat. . .you couldn't do that, but I would save Charles a trip if I could take you home. . . .

"You were getting out of the car when the Lord put this question in my mind, 'what is this business of being baptized in the Holy Spirit?' And you said, 'come to our home next Tuesday; we'll be discussing that.'

"Never have Ed and I agonized over a decision as this: whether to ask to receive or not.

"In yours and Charles' testimony on that April 25th night you answered all our questions (and my, we Baptists had a lot of them). (By the way, if you know of anyone that has a tape of your testimony on the Holy Spirit we would love to get a copy.)

"You prayed for me and I received my heavenly language. As we were leaving, you asked Ed if he had received (he hadn't) and bless your heart, you took us back into the den and you prayed for Ed. . .he gloriously received too! The Lord knew I would later have many doubts so, in His perfect timing He allowed me to witness Ed's beautiful experience to bolster my own faith. PTL.

"You and Charles were so kind to open up your home again on May 15th and we witnessed and received another miracle. . .being touched by His Spirit. Frances, when we got home Ed and I were still so filled with the Holy Spirit we were on cloud 9. At bedtime Ed prayed for me and I was 'slain in

Spirit.' We were amazed; then I prayed for Ed and touched him and he too was 'slain in the Spirit'. What does this mean?

"Thank you so much for allowing us to come to your home. Please, let us come again. Our two teen-age boys are asking about these experiences. It's all so new to us. We are praying that some time they too can come to one of your home meetings and you and Charles will pray with them and that they too will receive these same Heavenly Blessings. (Author's note: they did!)

"Now, I understand the feeling the Lord placed in my heart from the very beginning concerning you. You were to be involved in one of the biggest steps in our lives. When I think back over the events of the last few months and look at God's calendar of events I CAN ONLY SAY 'WOW'—Wonder of Wonders what the Lord has done for these Baptists.

"Thank you, thank you dear Jesus for sending Frances and Charles Hunter into our lives. We will never be the same.

"Praise God for what He's going to do in your life too!"

God has not limited the outpouring of His Holy Spirit on any particular denomination, but rather upon all the believers in all denominations who hunger and thirst. Praise God! The Report of the Special Committee on the work of the Holy Spirit to the 182nd General Assembly of the United Presbyterian Church in the United States of America, copyright 1970 has some interesting things to say about the charismatic movement: "We are glad to note the beginning of a breakdown of the barriers that have deprived us of fellowship with Pentecostal denominations. Believing that both of these are the result of the work of the Holy Spirit, we call on United Presbyterians to be sensitive and responsive to the insights and experiences of fellow Christians within all traditions." (Page 1)

"Our conclusion, based on a study of the language and analogies used by Paul, is that in I Corinthians he is speaking of a peculiar kind of utterance attained in prayer in which praise and adoration overflow in ways that transcend ordinary speech." (Page 6)

The final statement in the 55 page report states: "The subcommittee found no evidence of pathology in the movement. The movement was found to be dynamic, growing, and involving persons from practically every denomination, walk and station in life. Varied educational backgrounds, and personality patterns are present and the socio-economic status ranges from the uneducated through those in high executive positions carrying great responsibility in major corporations, in federal government and in the space effort." (Page 55)

In our home meetings, we have seen people from nearly every denomination receive the baptism. We have seen hunger in all denominations. On a recent tour, after one service, we saw members of 11 different denominations begin praising God in their special praise language after accepting the baptism with the Holy Spirit. Praise God He hasn't just selected one denomination!

The Pentecostal Evangel, May 7, 1972 has a very interesting article: "Something wonderful has happened in the church world in the past few years. Some describe it as a spiritual renewal, a return to primitive Christianity. Others call it a charismatic explosion. One theologian said it is nothing less than a revolution comparable in importance to the establishment of the original apostolic church and to the Protestant Reformation. It was indeed a spiritual explosion that brought the Church into being. The book of Acts, chapter two, describes the event by saying the believers 'were all filled with the Holy Spirit, and began to speak with other tongues as the Spirit gave them utterance.' That is exactly what has happened recently to thousands of Presbyterians, Baptists, Lutherans, Episcopalians, and people of other denominations. They have been filled with the Holy Spirit and now they magnify Christ in other tongues, speaking of the wonderful works of God in languages they never learned. It has revolutionized their lives."

We have seen people receive the baptism individually; we have also seen more than one hundred receive at one time.

Frances: One of the most humorous and blessed moments recently was a young lady who came running into a meeting I had just concluded saying "Oh, Mrs. Hunter, I want to be baptized with the Holy Spirit (and you know what Jesus did when she said that sincerely, don't you?). . .and I want Jesus to give me a heavenly". . .and not another word in English came out! Out of her mouth flowed a beautiful heavenly language and after about two or three minutes, she stopped and looked at me and said, "Is that speaking in tongues?" She had never heard it before. Her desire was for all God had for her, so Jesus baptized her the instant she asked!

How we praise God for the old line Pentecostals. They have been criticized by many (including us) for some of their ways, but where would the great move of the Holy Spirit be today if it had not been fanned and kept alive by many of those Pentecostals? They didn't have the vast number of teaching books that we have today concerning the ministry of the Holy Spirit, the baptism with the Holy Spirit, etc., but bless them, Lord, they did all they knew to do, and we "non-Pentecostals" kept our dignity. Thank you, "old line Pentecostals" for being great spiritual pioneers.

The beautiful part about this fabulous life in the Spirit is that it is available to all believers— young and old, Catholic, Protestant or Jew. Praise God!

Are you ready?

CHAPTER 13

HOW TO RECEIVE
THE BAPTISM WITH
THE HOLY SPIRIT

Before writing this chapter, we asked God for a simple truth that would communicate the importance of asking for a special "love" language. I think it's most interesting that He gave us Acts 2:1-4. "And when the day of Pentecost was fully come, they were all with one accord in one place. And suddenly there came a sound from heaven as of a rushing mighty wind, and it filled all the house where they were sitting. And there appeared unto them cloven tongues like as of fire, and it sat upon each of them. And they were all filled with the Holy Ghost, and began to speak with other tongues, as the Spirit gave them utterance." (KJV)

The dictionary defines cloven as "split or divided." A cloven tongue is a divided tongue, or a split tongue. And just what is a "split" or "divided" tongue? A tongue which is divided between the natural and the supernatural—a tongue which can speak either in the natural language or in a spiritual "unknown" language. And why was the super-natural manifestation "tongues" of fire? Because the tongue was the instrument through which the fire from heaven was to come, and so it is through your tongue that God wants to send the baptism of fire or the baptism with the Holy Spirit.

Just as salvation is a gift, being baptized with the Holy Spirit is a gift from God. Believe it or not, many people do not know how to accept a gift. We feel uncomfortable and stiff. We freeze a little. Neither of us understood how to become a Christian until we were taught. Someone had to tell us and show us how simple it was! We didn't understand it was just asking God to forgive our sins and then asking Jesus Christ to come into our lives!

Paul says, "Anyone who calls upon the name of the Lord will be saved. But how shall they ask Him to save them unless they believe in him? And how can they believe in him if they have never heard about him? And how can they hear about him unless someone tells them?" (Romans 10:13-15). Receiving the baptism works practically the same way. Unless someone tells you, how can you know? And just as salvation is simple, so is the Holy Spirit baptism equally easy to receive.

The first step is to "know" you're saved. To eliminate any doubt on this score, let's pray a simple little prayer right now.

"Lord Jesus, forgive my sins. I am sorry for every sin I have ever committed, including those I cannot remember. Forgive me for wrong attitudes and bitterness. I turn from them. I ask you to come into my life and to be the Lord of my life, not just my Saviour. Right now I ask you to take ALL of me as I give myself in total surrender to you. Thank you for coming into my life. I want to serve you the rest of my life. Amen."

Probably the most important thing to remember at this point is that you are asking this same Jesus to give you the power of the Holy Spirit! You are NOT seeking tongues! Keep this in mind. After asking Jesus to baptize you, you are going to accept, by faith, the Holy Spirit. Remember you do not have to struggle to receive the baptism, you only have to accept it simply by exercising your faith. Relax.

The baptism really consists of three steps. First, praying to be baptized; second, believing you are; third, stepping out in faith and accepting the privilege of speaking in the language the Holy Spirit gives you (". . .for they heard them speaking").

If you really believe that you can trust Jesus, through faith, to meet you as baptizer, you are now ready to be baptized with the Hoy Spirit and to receive your own special "praise" language. You receive the Holy Spirit by simply asking and accepting. Jesus said in Luke 11:13 "And if even sinful persons like yourselves give children what they need, don't you realize that your heavenly Father will do at least as much, and give the Holy Spirit to those who ask for him?" You may or may not at this particular time have a tremendous emotional response, but don't be concerned either way.

Remember we mentioned earlier what George

had said to us about Peter taking the first step out of the boat? Only then did Jesus make the water hard under him. You have to do the same thing.

You have to give God your voice and His Holy Spirit will give you the language. Remember it is *your* voice, and *you* must start speaking and the Holy Spirit will turn it into a real language of the Spirit.

Remember to praise God! More exciting things happen when you praise God than at any other time, because God inhabits the praises of His people. In just a minute we're going to ask you to praise God, BUT NOT IN ENGLISH. The Holy Spirit doesn't speak two languages at one time, so for right now forget about English. They will be funny sounding syllables, so don't worry whether or not they make sense, because to you, they won't, but to God it will be beautiful. Why will it be beautiful? Because the Holy Spirit has inspired the utterance.

To speak in your native language you must make a decision to speak and your mind must instruct your voice, mouth and tongue to utter the words needed to audibly express a message. Your voice must make sounds and your tongue and mouth must form the words in obedience to the instructions of your mind.

To speak in a language you don't know, your voice, mouth and tongue must still obey your new instructor, the Holy Spirit. There will be no reconstruction or redesign of your physical functions, and they will still perform their normal way in obedience to the Spirit. In the case of the unknown language, the Holy Spirit is the counsellor—the instructor, and it is He who tells these physical parts of the body what to say. YOU must give the sounds, but the Holy Spirit gives the language. YOU make the decision to speak and your mind tells your voice to speak, but the Holy Spirit furnishes the words.

We would like to make a statement right now which we feel is important for you to know. Those in the upper room were told by Jesus to tarry until the Holy Spirit had come. When He came, they were INSTANTLY baptized. We do *not* have to tarry, because the Holy Spirit is here, never having returned to heaven since Pentecost. That is why the moment you pray in faith believing, Jesus will baptize you with the Holy Spirit instantly! All you have to do is accept. And remember what you are accepting is the Holy Spirit who gives you the power to live the Christian life, the power to be a witness, the power Jesus promised when He returned to heaven. Remember also that the supernatural manifestation of speaking in tongues is not the baptism. It is the result of the baptism. Too often people seek the result, and not the baptism, and have problems because of this.

Again, let us remind you to relax. You can't speak English or your native language very well if you are tense and have your teeth clenched together, so just relax and believe. Are you ready to pray? Well, then, let's just pray a simple little prayer together.

"Lord Jesus, I love you with all of my heart.
I want to be the person you want me to be,

so I'm asking you to give me the power you gave to the disciples on the day of Pentecost. I'm going to give you my voice and ask you to make the air hard under the sounds of my voice, just like you made the water hard under Peter's feet. Jesus, I ask you to baptize me right now with the Holy Spirit and I thank you in advance for the language you're going to give me." Amen.

Do you really believe Jesus is with you right now, wanting to baptize you with the Holy Spirit? We do, and because we do, we're asking you right now to believe this prayer as we lay "hands" on you in faith through the pages of this book: "Jesus, baptize this Christian right now with the Holy Spirit. Fill him up all the way from the bottom to the top."

Just sit there a minute until you know that Jesus has baptized you. Now will you lift your hands in praise and worship to God? "So I want men everywhere to pray with holy hands lifted up to God, free from sin and anger and resentment" (I Timothy 2:8). Just praise God silently for a moment.

Now, just breathe in the Holy Spirit (take a deep breath) and as you let your breath out, let it slide out easily with a long continuation of different sounds. Remember this is one time you must come as a little child and be willing to make simple little sounds. Keep your mind on Jesus!

Hallelujah! Do you hear that beautiful praise language to God?

Who baptized you?

JESUS!

The instant the Holy Spirit used your voice, you KNEW it was real, didn't you? Praise God.

Mark 16:17. . . "And these signs shall follow them that believe; In my name shall they cast out devils; they shall speak with new tongues. . ."

CHAPTER 14

WHAT COMES AFTER
THE BAPTISM?

ACTION! That's what comes after the baptism! Praise God with your new language every opportunity you have! I pray in the Spirit as I do all my household chores because there's lots to praise God for there! I praise Him for the electric dishwasher I have! As I scrub the stove, I praise Him in the Spirit for letting me cook on a stove that doesn't require me to go out and chop down trees to get it heated up. I praise God for my electric vacuum cleaner and never mind the task at all.

Charles prays in the Spirit when he's driving to and from work. He and the Lord have a most wonderful time. This way he never minds how many times he gets stopped by the red lights—it just gives him that much more time to praise God!

The more you pray in the Spirit, the more fluent your language will become. Somehow I have never been able to understand how God uses something as "silly" as this, but HE sure does. God said He would use the foolish things to confound the wise! Don't try to understand it, just take advantage of this beautiful blessing the Lord has given you.

And then sing, sing, sing in the Spirit. We've discovered this does more to cement the reality of tongues than anything else. Just let God give you the tune and the words. You'll probably notice when you sing in the Spirit that your voice will be considerably higher than it normally is. It is really great to have the beautiful freedom of praise to God in song! He enjoys it because I'm sure we must sound like an angel choir to Him. Charles and I sing in the Spirit together in bed, around the house or in the car. We have often walked down the corridors in airports arm in arm after a real exciting meeting, and the power of the Lord is so strong we're about to "bust." Our own English vocabulary just doesn't express how we feel, so we begin praising God in the Spirit, singing softly. We have often been stopped by the people who can't hear us, but who say, "I've never seen two people as happy as you two!"

Why shouldn't we be happy; we're praising God in His special language! You just can't possibly pray to God in the Spirit without your own spirits being lifted! Hallelujah!

Right now we want to remind you that Satan himself will come charging up to you saying, "That's not real! You're making that up yourself!" Rebuke him in the name of Jesus! Recently we heard someone say, "Isn't that just like the devil, taking credit for the 'praise' language?" He's so afraid of the power of the baptism with the Holy Spirit, he tries to take the credit himself and let people say tongues are of the devil. Almost everyone has a quick visit from Satan because he doesn't want you to have this added power. I did, and for a moment I thought "Am *I* doing this?" (Don't you try to take credit for it either!) And then I remembered one thing! Who did I ask to baptize me? Jesus!

Who baptized me?

JESUS!

Who baptized you?

JESUS!...And don't you ever forget that!

So many things have happened to us since we opened our hearts to the fullness of God's Holy Spirit, we are out of breath! Isn't it wonderful to know that we can all share in this? We both feel we wouldn't trade our lives with anyone! Hallelujah! Jesus is more real than ever before, and we're just loving God more and more all the time.

God has allowed us to get into some real exciting spots and each time He has rescued us by His power! The first time we ever shared the news that we had received the baptism, 26 people came up to be prayed for. Twelve were men and fourteen were women. We wanted to see how someone who knew what to do ministered the baptism! There wasn't another person there with us. Both of us instantly cried out to God because we knew we couldn't do a thing on our own, and Jesus baptized all 26! We learned real fast you don't have to be an expert, you just have to trust God, and He will never let you down! He will work through any willing vessel.

Recently the Lord has given us so much extra boldness we can hardly believe it. There is nothing worse than a reformed alcoholic, unless it's a re-

formed cigaretteholic! And that's what I am. When
Jesus delivered me from cigarettes shortly after I
became a Christian, He did it well. He took every desire away from me and no longer was I chained to
this tool of Satan. For years I have shared the story
of how God broke every fetter, and each time I have
shared the story I have said, "I'm not telling you
what to do, I'm only telling you what God did in my
life. If you've got a problem, it's between you and
God, not between you and me!"

Recently the Lord's been making me eat those
words! All of a sudden He's reminded me that time
is drawing short, and that a Christian doesn't have a
right to waste his time and his body smoking, and a
Christian shouldn't have a right to spend his money
on such instruments of Satan. And He's reminded
me that many of the smokers don't realize their body
is the "temple of God." They should do nothing to
defile it. "Know ye not that ye are the temple of God,
and that the Spirit of God dwelleth in you? If any
man defile the temple of God, him shall God destroy; for the temple of God is holy, which temple ye
are" (I Corinthians 3:16-17 KJV).

The Holy Spirit has begun moving me to people
who have cigarettes in their pockets and purses.
God is causing me to take a stand on the body being
the Holy Temple of God, and the results are gratify-
ing!

At a recent luncheon meeting, the Lord revealed to me that a number of women had cigarettes
in their purses. I stopped right in the middle of my
talk, and shared with them about the way the Lord

dealt with me on cigarettes! Then I asked everyone who had cigarettes to take them out, and lift them to God, and crush them as I cursed them in the name of Jesus. The number of packages of cigarettes left on tables, in water glasses, and on the floor, would have restocked a store. I also added an extra little prayer and said, "Jesus, may they vomit and get violently ill if they ever dare smoke again!"

Not everyone believes God will answer a little prayer like that, but I do! A young girl said to her mother right after I prayed, "I don't like her. She hasn't any right to tell me not to smoke. I enjoy it and I'm going to keep on smoking." With that she left the meeting. The mother came running up to me and said, "What shall I do?" I merely said, "Praise God! He's working in her life."

The daughter ran out of the plush restaurant which was on the second floor of a building, ran down to the street floor, lit a cigarette, and "something" knocked her to the floor! Those behind her ran up and all she could say was, "I'm so sick, I'm so sick!" They ran to get her mother who looked the situation over and then came running back upstairs to where Charles and I were and told me what happened. She asked what she should do. I said, "Praise God! The Holy Spirit is doing a great work!"

Another woman left the meeting, and as she walked down the elegant hallway of the building, she lit a cigarette and VOMITED all over the carpet! Hallelujah! Instantly seven more women came running, almost throwing their cigarettes at Charles and me, asking to be prayed for! We didn't see another person light a cigarette from then on.

And so it goes!

On a recent trip to Albuquerque, New Mexico, the Lord laid it on my heart the first night that the cigarettes needed to go. At the mid-way part of the service I shared the above story with them. We asked everyone to bring their cigarettes to the altar. Before the night was over, Charles and I were standing "ankle deep" in cigarettes which had been broken right in half, and thrown on the floor!

One of the most exciting things that happened didn't just concern cigarettes! One young man of Mexican descent came forward with his cigarettes, but the Lord revealed his real problem was alcohol, and not cigarettes! I asked him if it wasn't really alcohol that bound him, and he was honest and said, "Yes." He accepted Jesus as Saviour and Lord, then we prayed for deliverance from alcohol and cigarettes. The power of God went through him and he looked up and said, "Something's happened to me in here!" He pointed to his stomach. Then he added: "I'm going home and pour all my whiskey out!" I hadn't said a word about that, but God had spoken to him. Jesus snapped the chains of alcohol which had bound him for 27 years! And He did it instantly!

An older Mexican man came forward crying at this time. He could not speak one word of English, and hadn't understood a word I'd said, but the young man who had just been delivered from alcohol and cigarettes interpreted for his father and me as the father said, "I want to be saved." Praise God, His Holy Spirit came through the language barrier and brought conviction to his heart! Then God used the son who had just been delivered to translate the prayer of repentance to the father. Hallelujah!

The power of God was so strong, others began coming to the altar asking to be saved, and we hadn't even gotten around to that part of the service yet! Praise God! Many received the baptism that night and were gloriously filled.

Another man who had smoked a pipe for 37 years was delivered, and the next day his family had "burial" services for his other 5 pipes!

God is moving by His spirit and almost everyone who was delivered said, "God has been dealing with me about smoking," or "I decided to stop tonight," or "I threw my cigarettes away just before I came in the church." God had already done the work before I ever got there, and all the people needed was confirmation that it was God working.

God is freeing people from the slavery of fear, doubt, worry, anxiety and hopelessness through the power of His Holy Spirit. Couples have come to us in complete desperation, knowing they were saved, but knowing also they were defeated Christians, because the real joy wasn't there! After receiving the baptism, their lives have gone straight up to victory. The Holy Spirit gives you the ability to conquer all the things that bind you! He sets you free in a way you could never imagine before it happens! God said He would give us all power over the enemy.

A learned Christian psychologist who is the chairman of the Division of Education and Psychology at one of the leading universities in Texas recently states: "I can explain it psychologically, sociologically, and emotionally, but I can't explain what happens to me inside when I pray in the Spirit!" He and his wife received the baptism at our home and their lives have been turned right side up with the new power, joy and enthusiasm.

There is a definite "revving" up of your understanding where reading the Bible is concerned. The scriptures almost leap out from the pages and it seems the thirsting for God becomes more and more intense as the flame of the Holy Spirit burns hotter and hotter in your life!

Souls become important! More important than they've ever been before. After the baptism, the longing within your own heart is intensified to see more and more people come to know Jesus! And the power you have now received allows you to become an instrument God uses in their lives. Hallelujah!

Time becomes more productive! The Holy Spirit is efficient. Now that you have been energized by His power, He craves action, and you will discover a change in the way you use your time. In God's economy, time is precious, and is running out. There are still so many people who need to know about Jesus. You'll find more efficiency in your housework and your business life to enable you to do what God wants you to do! He'll give you that extra time to get into the Word with more energy than you've ever had before!

New things will happen when you talk to people! The power of the Holy Spirit will come through you in ways you won't even know. One of the first services Charles and I held, after we had announced we had received the baptism, was full of surprises! We were speaking at a retreat type situation, and had just read a scripture when a message in tongues came out! It was probably the most electrifying message I've ever heard. It happened to be in a group who do not believe in nor practice the gifts of the Spirit, and all God whispered to me was, "Let me do it my way." The message was the very heart cry of God Himself calling upon people not to turn away from His love. It so moved the entire congregation that tears broke out all over the place. This was followed by an unholy scream, the likes of which I've never heard before nor since.

I nearly fell off the platform, because I had never dealt with a situation like this, but God kept whispering, "Let me do it my way, let me do it MY way," so I DID NOTHING. The woman who had screamed told us later the power of God was so strong she saw her own son in hell, being consumed by fire. We have been told it was Satan himself who could not stand the extreme power of the Holy Spirit which had engulfed the entire meeting.

We continued to let God have His way, and as a result, almost all of those at the retreat came forward to rededicate their lives to God. Barriers which had existed between people were broken down as the Holy Spirit hovered over us. People began crying and saying, "Somehow I know there's more—how do I find it?"

We had said practically nothing! The Holy

Spirit had done it all. I felt like a spectator rather than a speaker! God's Holy Spirit had used an empty vessel through which He could move to bring hundreds to a new relationship with Jesus!

At a meeting in northern Michigan recently a most unique thing happened which I'd like to share with you, just to show how God's Holy Spirit is being poured out these last days. We had just concluded a 3 day city-wide crusade at a high school auditorium. Everyone had gone home. The clean-up committee was folding up the chairs and putting them away. All the lights were turned off. Charles and I were ministering to a few people who were still left on the stage when through the one door which was still unlocked came a man who had attended one or two of our meetings there.

He was obviously drunk, but walked up and said, "I don't know why I'm here, but I want to tell you a story!" He had been sitting in a bar with another friend when all of a sudden "something" made him get up off the bar stool and go outside. He thought he was going to go to another bar across the street, but "something" took him to his car and put him inside. This same "something" then made him drive the car to the high school auditorium where we were. He said there was nothing he could do except to follow this "something" which was directing him. He stood there, a picture of loneliness and despair, looking so lost and forlorn. Then he repeated, "I don't even know why I'm here!"

I said, "I do," and then cried out, "God, save Frank!" At that instant, the Holy Spirit broke him, and he began to sob as though his heart was break-ing. I then cursed alcohol in his life, and through his tears he cried, "Jesus, I'll never touch alcohol or to-bacco again as long as I live!" Then he took the cigar out of his pocket and broke it right in two!

God softly whispered, "He needs the baptism, too!" so I just kept my hands on him and said, "Jesus, baptize him with the Holy Spirit," and im-mediately between the tears and sobs, he began to speak in tongues! Hallelujah! In a matter of four or five minutes, God had reached down and saved him, Jesus had delivered him from alcoholism and to-bacco, and he had been baptized with the Holy Spirit! God is fabulous!

The mighty rushing wind which is sweeping the country has gone into every nook and cranny in our great country, and probably in the entire world. People are being delivered from all kinds of prob-lems as if God's extra powerful vacuum cleaner was turned on them alone. People are seeking the power of God, and are becoming aware of what the power of the Holy Spirit is really all about and how we need it to be victorious in our Christian lives! Praise God for his promises.

A young man with long hair and an immacu-lately trimmed beard came to me at a meeting re-cently and asked for the baptism with the Holy Spirit. I asked him if he was positive he was saved, and if he knew Jesus as his personal Saviour, and he answered he was positive about this, but he needed something more in his life. I just simply asked Jesus to meet his need; and He did, so the young man went away rejoicing!

Charles and I had ministered to the needs of many people after the meeting was over, and we were just gathering up our Bibles, when four young people came back into the restaurant. I saw the young man who had received the baptism earlier in the evening take a deep breath, really straighten his shoulders, put his hand in his coat pocket, take something out, and then very deliberately and carefully walk toward me. With his hand outstretched he said, "After the baptism, I had to come back and give this to you."

I looked at what he had given me. It was the zig-zag papers to wrap around marijuana, but that wasn't all! Carefully hidden in the wrappers was a "fix" of heroin! How we praise God for what He can do! He told me he had been an addict for 15 years, but after receiving the baptism, he KNEW the habit was gone. Hallelujah!

CHAPTER 15

THE SECOND HOT LINE

I often have to laugh when I think of the stomachache I received when George said to me, "You've got one hot line to heaven, wouldn't you like to have two?" . . .and he was so right, because that extra hot line can really give you a lot of additional prayer power! One of the most exciting things we've found with praying in the Spirit is that as people's names and faces come across your mind, you can instantly lift them up in the Spirit, knowing full well that the Holy Spirit within you is praying just exactly the prayer that needs to be prayed! Sometimes I wonder what a particular person's needs are as they flit across the T.V. screen of my mind, but I know that God knows their needs and He has put their image in my mind so that I could pray for them, so why should I worry? I just go ahead and lift that individual in prayer.

After Charles and I had doubled our prayer life with our second Hot Line to Heaven, we of course began to notice more and more prayer answers. God began doing more and more of the impossible, and we were convinced over and over again of the extra blessing of being able to pray in the Spirit as well as in English.

. . .and then came the week of June 1, 1972.

We had been in Portland, Oregon at a Regional Convention of the Full Gospel Businessmen's Fellowship International, and while there we heard a speaker ask everyone to fast and pray one day a week for the President, the Cabinet, the members of the House and Senate. This really struck home to both Charles and me. When we arrived back in Houston we decided to fast and pray for the executives of our nation. We selected the very next day as the one when all three of us, Charles, Joan and I, would join together in this special type of prayer.

We started off the day the same as we do all others, saying, "Jesus, I love you," and then, "Well, Lord, what fabulous things do you have for us today?" Try taking the name of Jesus on your lips the very first thing when you wake up (even before you open your eyes) and see what happens to you when you do! Then we got up and started our day of fasting and prayer.

Some people don't drink water when they fast, but we did. We started the day off with a glass of water and prayer, asking God if He would mind if we included my son Tom in with the prayers for the nation. Apparently He didn't mind so as we drank the water, we just lifted Tom in prayer and said three little words, "Jesus, save Tom!"

We might have added more than that, but we had recently heard Ralph Marinacci tell about his large Italian family, and how one by one they all accepted Jesus Christ as their Saviour and Lord. Mama Marinacci was first, and then Papa Marinacci, and then one by one all the little Marinaccis, except Ralph. Ralph was the stubborn one. He played the trumpet in a night club and didn't want any of this "religious" stuff. He really ran when any of his family spoke about Christ. His sister Angie was really burdened for him, and every night when Ralph came home from playing in the honky tonks, Angie was on her knees praying just three little words, "Jesus, save Ralph!" After a while, this got Ralph so irritated and annoyed he just couldn't stand it, so he went out and got himself saved!

Just the very simple way Angie asked for his salvation impressed me, so every time we got hungry on our first fast day, we'd run to the water faucet in the kitchen, and as we'd drink a glass of water, we'd say, "Jesus, save Tom!" Just three little words, but oh, how important they were. We decided if it had worked so well in the Marinacci family, it should work in ours as well.

Maybe I should tell you the beginning of the story before I go any further. I didn't become a Christian until Tom was 21 years of age, which meant he had been raised in a non-Christian home. And mothers and dads, let me assure you there's a price you pay when you raise your children in a non-Christian home. Somehow or other, when we raise a child without the fear and admonition of the Lord, things can happen in their lives that shouldn't. I willingly take all the responsibility upon my shoulders, because Tom was not raised in a Christian home, so how could he know what God expected of him?

I found Jesus at the ripe old age of 49 and things really began to happen! Somehow or other when I met Jesus, I didn't see a "half-way" Jesus—I saw it had to be Jesus all the way or not at all. I honestly believe God opened the windows of heaven and gave me a little peek to see what eternity was all about, and I've never wanted anything except more, more, more of God from that day on! Praise God, our daughter Joan accepted Christ shortly after I did, but Tom was no longer living at home, and any Christian influence I might have exerted was lost.

If you've read my book, HOT LINE TO HEAVEN, you'll remember the dedication page which says: "Dedicated with great love to my son Tom. . .Some people accept Christ easily—they hear the Gospel and don't put up a great struggle. Then there is the rebel who fights every inch of the way. Such is my son Tom."

The closer I got to God, the faster he ran from God. The mother who had always been so much fun was now a big pain to her son. I remember when he told me, "You're no fun any more—you don't drink, you don't smoke, you don't dance, you don't tell dirty jokes. . .you're just not fun to be around any more!" Somehow he failed to understand that Jesus Christ had transformed my life and made a new creature out of me. . .a new creature who didn't need the things of the world. . .a new creature who dis-covered the things of God were far more exciting than any of the things she'd ever been involved with before!

Tom couldn't see it that way, and in spite of everything I said, the more I fell in love with Jesus, the faster Tom ran in the other direction. I tried for a long time to do the work of the Holy Spirit, but finally one day I gave up and just gave him to God and said, "God, he's yours—not mine. I GIVE HIM TO YOU AND I'LL NEVER TAKE HIM BACK. Do whatever it takes, but save him!" And from that day on, the worry was no longer mine. There were times when I had to slap my hand because I wanted to take the problem back, but God reminded me that I had given it to Him, so I just left it there.

Over the years I saw Tom running as fast as he could in the opposite direction. Sometimes I wondered if it wasn't done deliberately to aggravate me. People have asked me, "Aren't you embarrassed to run all over the country telling people that Jesus Christ is the answer to life when your own son behaves the way he does?" I had a standard answer for them! "Just looking at my own son has convinced me more than anything else that Jesus Christ is the only answer!" Tom hadn't even called me "Mother" for three years, and is there anything that hurts much more than to have your own child call you by your first name instead of Mother?

For several weeks before we left to go to Abilene, Texas, we had been receiving phone calls from Tom and his wife constantly. Their marriage was really on the rocks, and it just didn't seem as if there was any hope for it. They would call us, and while the three of us were on the extensions in our home, Tom and his wife would proceed to fight with each other. For some reason or other I became a little robot and could only say "Jesus is the only way— there is no other answer for your problems." It was as though God had blanked out my mind completely. I must have sounded just like a little parrot because I could say absolutely nothing else! Maybe I would change the wording a little and say, "Nothing is ever going to be right until you learn to put Jesus first in your life and your marriage." There was not another word of advice that could come out. But then, what other good advice was there to give? NONE!

The heathen could have advised, "Keep the house cleaner so he won't have to walk through the garbage to get in the house at night," or "Why don't you try being polite to her, and more considerate," but this would only have been patching an old wineskin with a new patch—the infection would have just broken out someplace else. So all we kept saying was, "Jesus is the only answer!" or "Until you are willing to turn to God, there is no way!"

Praise God He teaches us lessons all along the way, and not just one lesson, but a lot of them. Long ago we had learned to praise God for *all* things, and when we began to realize that Tom and his wife were really having serious problems, we really had to praise the Lord. Every time we would hang up the telephone after a call which made us feel there was absolutely no hope because things were such a mess, we would all join in the living room and say, "Praise the Lord. Thank you Jesus. Keep on making them miserable until they get right with you. Lord, just make them so miserable they can't stand themselves until they look up and see you, just waiting there with your arms outstretched to draw them into your kingdom." I was just wondering how many times we have said, "Praise the Lord. . .Thank you Jesus for making them miserable" when our hearts were really breaking. Isn't it wonderful, though, how God puts all of His Holy Word into action when we are obedient?

Things really continued to get worse and worse, and just before we left for Abilene, Tom and his wife separated. We said, "Praise the Lord." He was living in an apartment by himself on one side of town, and she got a job in a bar in order to feed the kids. One night while she was at work, he went in and took the bed and T.V. set. See what Satan can do when he gets his grimy hands on people!

When his wife called us and said that Tom had made off with the bed, we said, "Praise the Lord, give thanks for all things" even if you don't have a bed to sleep in." (We discovered later he had left her an old bed.) Then we added another, "Thank you, Jesus" for the fact that the three kids didn't have a T.V. to watch. All of us met in our Texas room after that phone call and really praised the Lord. Charles and I sang in the Spirit, and just generally had a marvelous time praising God. Again we prayed that God would make them so miserable they couldn't stand it any longer. Many people would never pray that way, but some people have to go all the way to rock bottom before they can look up and see Jesus, and we felt the sooner the better!

I thought we'd starve to death before the end of the fast! It was a day when we prayed constantly and were all so very close to Him and so ever mindful of His presence.

Thursday we left for Abilene. We were excited about being there because it was the first time we had ever been on the same program with George Otis. We were really excited about the three of us being together.

The Lord had graciously allowed Joan to be with us on this trip, and on the way—now watch how God works—all three of us (Charles, Joan and I) "happened" to end up reading Proverbs in the Living Bible. I don't believe it "happened"—I believe it was God who had us reading where we were. As we got farther and farther along, we began laughing at various places in the Living Bible and finally decided that God had written Proverbs just for Tom!

By the time I got to the 10th Chapter, I knew that God was saying some very important things to me at that time, so I began to write some of these things down (in ink). I read the first verse of Chapter 10: "Happy is the man with a level headed son; *sad the mother of a rebel.*" My mind flashed back to the dedication of the book HOT LINE TO HEAVEN, so opposite this verse I wrote the word "TOM". Just alongside the verse I wrote "EXCEPT FOR JESUS." I had given him to God, so the worry wasn't mine, but I sure would have been sad if it hadn't been for that!

I continued reading and Proverbs 11:21 spoke to me in a special way: "You can be very sure that the evil man will not go unpunished forever. . ." My heart tightened up at that moment because I knew that if Jesus would come back right then, my own son would not go unpunished, and no mother wants to see her son spend eternity in hell! I don't believe hell was ever such a reality to me as it was at that moment because I could see my own son being devoured by its flames. And what a feeling of complete helplessness, because I knew there was nothing I could do about it. That was a horrible moment as I looked at Tom's bleak future without God and I looked at his eternity. I had never seen Tom's eternal destiny as clearly as I saw it that day, and I didn't like what I saw!

I read on: "And you can also be very sure that God will rescue the children of the godly!"

My heart almost jumped out of my body! Look at this beautiful promise of God! He promised he would save the children of the godly. And what had I ever done to deserve the word "godly?" Nothing, absolutely nothing. It had all been done for me at Calvary. I really got excited, because never before had I seen Tom's eternal destiny in such a light as this. I was ecstatic! Alongside this I wrote three tiny words—"JESUS SAVE TOM!" All of my Bibles of all translations have Tom's name written alongside many verses, but this one really spoke to me that day high in the sky. I showed it to Charles, then to Joan, and the three of us claimed Tom's soul again.

Tom had called us just before this asking us to

send him $500 because he had quit his job as a printer. He said he "wasn't about to get his hands dirty" and I asked him who was going to feed his wife and three children, but he didn't seem to worry. (I found out later he wanted to use the money to make a down payment on a Cadillac. . .we didn't send the money!)

Then I came to 12:9. "It is better to get your hands dirty—and eat, than to be too proud to work—and starve." Opposite this, guess whose name I wrote. TOM, of course. We had a real good laugh over that verse.

Then I continued on to the 13th chapter, second verse. "The good man wins his case by careful argument; the evil-minded only wants to fight." And Tom really loved to fight! He'd rather fight than switch any day.

Now watch what the Lord had me write in my Bible that day. I wrote "TOM," but I added something new and very special. For the very first time I wrote the initials "(B.C.)" (Before Christ) after Tom's name. I continued on, and we laughed at many of the verses, feeling they were especially for Tom.

Then I came to 15:19. "A lazy fellow has trouble all through life; (and above this I wrote "TOM B.C."). And isn't that really the truth? A lazy fellow who doesn't accept Christ because he thinks he can get along without God really has a miserable time in life, and will continue to have a miserable time. Right after that came the rest of the verse. ". . .the good man's path is easy!" I thought, how true this statement is, because even though we have problems after we become a Christian, we have the Problem Solver, and Jesus tells us to cast all our burdens upon Him and He will give us rest, so think how easy our life really is when we trust God all the way. Right after that little verse, I really stepped out in faith and wrote "TOM (A.C.)" (After Christ).

Never before had I ever had enough faith to write that, or even think it, but God was really working, so that's exactly what I wrote (in ink, so I couldn't erase it either). Little did any of us realize what God was preparing for us!

We arrived in Abilene, and were excited about seeing George, but didn't get to see him until the next morning at breakfast. He sat down beside us, but didn't stay long. I didn't realize what had happened until about an hour and a half later. When George returned he didn't say a thing, but showed me a little note which said "Call Tom Steder," and the Miami telephone number listed beside it.

For one minute Satan jabbed me with a little fear dart concerning Tom and his family because I knew the trouble that was brooding over their home. I said, "Did you call them?" George answered with one word, "Yes!" My heart really skipped a beat! I finally got out the words, "What's the matter?!" George just looked at me and said, "Nothing!" And yet I knew there was more. My mind flashed in about 50 different directions at one time. Finally George just said, "Nothing's the matter. . .Tom and his wife both just accepted Christ!"

My cup overflowed! Neither Charles, Joan or I

said a single word! We couldn't! Our joy knew no bounds, as tears flowed from all of us. God saw to it that we were all together in this great moment of joy and fulfillment of the scriptures,"And you can also be very sure that God will rescue the children of the godly." I whispered, "Thank you, Jesus" from the depths of my soul and then turned in my Bible opposite the above verse and wrote: "Double portion, June 2, 1972, Patty, too!"

God not only granted our request, He gave us a double portion as well! How we all rejoiced! "Thank the Lord for all the glorious things he does: proclaim them to the nations. Sing his praises and tell everyone about his miracles. Glory in the Lord; O worshipers of God, rejoice! Search for him and for his strength and keep on searching" (Psalms 105:1-4).

The Lord immediately dealt with all of us concerning bringing Tom and Patty to Abilene to share their newfound happiness. George paid to bring them to Abilene, for even though we felt we should, we knew the Holy Spirit had said to give him this pleasure, so within two hours of their momentous decision to turn their lives and marriage over to God, reservations were made and they came to Abilene.

What a joyous reunion! God wanted our family to be together at that beautiful and holy time when we were all united under His banner of love!

Tom hadn't called me "Mother" for years, but once he joined the Royal Family of God, that word came right back into his vocabulary. The first words he said were, "Hello, Mother, you were right!" And Charles became Dad. Hallelujah!

George Otis introduced them at the banquet on Saturday night and I feel his words are worth repeating, because so many of us try to make our children just like we are, or hope to be, and we can't do it.

George said: "It's a hard thing to be a son and a daughter-in-law of somebody like Frances and Charles Hunter. God made every single one of us with unique fingerprints, unique features on our face, different tone in our voice. . .Everyone of us is utterly unique. God the great Creator made you and made Tom and Patty, and then he broke the mold! He's got only one Tom. Tom is TOM, more than he is the son of Frances Hunter, and my son George is George more than he is my son. God longs for each and every one of us. And so I'm delighted that these two would come here to grace this particular gathering of the body of Christ."

Tom said: "Well, you know like we'd been married for quite a while, and it was a pretty rocky road by ourselves. Well, you know. . .There's a couple of snickers out there, and you really don't know what I mean. Really. I mean we made a mess of it by ourselves and we've decided that we can't do it, so we're going to take God with us, and He can do it!"

Then Patty said: "Well, like Tom said, we really blew it. We blew it bad! (Tom added: "As much as we love each other, we blew it.") And it finally got to the point where we knew we couldn't make it—there was no way—unless we turned to God. We just want His arms around us all the time in all ways."

Did you hear the words that came back to me? Almost exactly the same thing I had been saying all along! God stamped the words in their minds. Praise His Holy Name! Many times as parents we back down when the storms really get rough around our children, but praise God He didn't let us give them any advice similar to what the heathen would have said, but only what He wanted, that the answer was to turn to God.

For all you mothers who may read this, and who have children who are lost, I pray right now that you will lay your hand upon this page and claim the promise that I claimed, "And you can also be very sure that God will rescue the children of the godly."

"Father, we praise you for giving us hope. We praise you for giving us faith to believe that what you have written in your Holy Word is true. We praise you because you have made provision for our children. We thank you that you have promised to rescue the children of the godly. And we thank you for the fact we know we are godly only by your grace and love and mercy. Thank you for saving us and making us your children. Now, Father, as hands are laid on the printed words of this page, may you hear every mother's heart that cries out, 'Jesus, save _____ !'

And now Father, thank you, thank you, thank you, for saving Tom and giving us a double portion, because we were praying for Patty, too! And thank you, Lord, for saving the children of the godly who claim that promise right now!"